Philip Hodgins was born in 1959 and died
in 1995 of leukaemia. His awards include the
Bicentennial Poetry Book Award, the New South
Wales Premier's Award, the Grace Leven Prize and
the National Book Council Poetry Prize.
He is survived by his wife Janet and their two
children, Anna and Helen.

New Selected Poems

Philip Hodgins

DUFFY & SNELLGROVE
SYDNEY

The publishers wish to thank Peter Goldsworthy, Jamie Grant,
Robert Gray and Les Murray for allowing us to republish
poems to or about Philip Hodgins in this book.

Published by Duffy & Snellgrove in 2000
PO Box 177 Potts Point NSW 2011 Australia
info@duffyandsnellgrove.com.au

An earlier edition of this book was published by
Angus and Robertson in 1997

Distributed by Pan Macmillan

Thanks to Pete Sharp for the hostel story in 'Second Thoughts on
The Georgics' and to *The Sydney Morning Herald*.
Blood and Bone (1986), *Animal Warmth* (1990), *Up On All
Fours* (1993), *Dispossessed* (1994) and *Things Happen* (1995)
published by HarperCollins Publishers. *Down the Lake with Half
a Chook* (1988) published by ABC Enterprises.
The poem 'The Discs' previously appeared in *Animal Warmth*
with the title 'A Prayer'.

The cover, designed by Alex Snellgrove, incorporates
the author's handwriting.
Typeset by Maggie Cooper
Printed by Griffin Press

ISBN 1 875989 75 7

visit our website: www.duffyandsnellgrove.com.au

Contents

For *la famiglia:*
Janet, Anna, Helen,
Hattie, Margie, Rob,
Stefano, Donata, Hartley,
Jennie, Arthur, Dugald,
Roddis, Liz, and the
Port Phillip Gentleman

From *Blood and Bone*

Platform Verse

a man stands single
on a railway station platform
alone with the smell of his own body:
the sun is low

his shadow is bigger than he
the wind interferes with him:
a train comes
its shadow blocks out the shadow of the man

its smell blocks out the smell
of his socks and armpits:
the train catches its breath and creaks
and rolls right out of town

Room 1 Ward 10 West 12/11/83

Today they said there was no cure,
that all this stuff could do no good.
They hadn't spelled it out before,
and only now I understood

what one uncommon word had done
to human gestures never made.
Tonight the dying has begun.
There is no cure for blood gone bad.

Those friends who've seen me in this room
in time will see me to the earth
and stand around in groups and say
expected things about this death.

But will they think I chose to play
my most important piece too soon?

The sun begins
beyond the not-forgotten farm.
Two hours of work
before high school I kawasaki dogless away from sleep
to end cowsleep in a glazed paddock.
Although obscured by gumtrees thronged along the creek,
I see the light is badly bruised and in one spot
it even bleeds.
An ibis crosses my ken
old-fashioned as a pterodactyl.
Water hens duck into the otherworld rushes.
Dawn air reddens my don't-leave-me grip and freezes
my face on fire while I pogo tufts and ruts,
buzzingly sorting out stones.
Arrival has no effect.
They remain levant and couchant in join-the-dots
dispersal. I go to the nearest sleeper,
a honey jersey, and beat her drum.
She collapses up and awake. I go further
into the paddock and forget about cows
finding instead a ghostly breakfast tableau.
Beautifully clean mushrooms
made gregarious by night
hold white above the staining green.
Each group a reject dinner set, some chipped,
some the wrong size.
I take the best,
lifting them slowly as a saucer of milk,
and feed them to my duckbilled cap
remembering their power.
(Once, after rain, I found one
punching through a disused tennis court
with a shard of the old asphalt poised on top.)
Ignoring not-there-yesterday
golden gobstoppers and Pine Gap puffballs, I come back

5

over simple speed traps,
primal screaming at cows.
Not listening, udders up, they funnel
into the lane,
some syringing shaky milk-graphs onto the dust.
Tails lazily trying to be everywhere
herald the beginning of flies.
The unfinished tapestry moves by habit in easy,
muffled commotion to a fixed finishing order
and nagging relief.
I follow them with my gift.

Room 1 Ward 10 West 23/11/83

Wordless afternoon
before my friends
for all their reasons
look in on me

They have time
to choose the words
they would
like me to hear

I am attached
to a dark
bag of blood
leaking near me

I have time
to choose the words
I am
likely to need

At twenty-four
there are many words
and this one
death

A Palinode

My second childhood has begun
but the rhythms and the rhymes aren't quite right.
The way my cells increase
is not unlike the vague, unbitten child
reaching up to childhood's end.
But with one difference.
My half a bucketful of blood
is filled with rumours of an early death
and I am alone in a room
full of dying flowers.
I think it is the body's palinode
and as far as I can see there is no God.

Leaving Hospital

There was no joy in leaving. Nothing was resolved.
Blood and bone were shot and death had shown
a way with words beyond the usual sophistry.
Wounded by prognosis I had brought people together
and encouraged conversation. It didn't help.
The right debates were held alone each night
after the chatter of the last drug trolley down
the polished corridor. It was impossible to match
death's vocabulary. I gave up and got ready to go.
No amount of speechmaking could reassemble
those disparate friends or justify all that fuss.
On the steps I felt the hospital's immensity
behind me. I thought of how this blood, this
volition would bring me back here to die
in stages of bitterness and regret. I turned around.
The doors are open.

Catharsis

Beyond incorrigible death, childhood's small killings
are still there blinking up at me as I hoisted the bale
of hay. All a tabby mother's love and cunning were
undone by the necessity of feeding out. I counted seven.
Their softness began to stir as I took them away
from the haystack's labyrinth. They caught on my jumper
like roses. Behind the machinery shed I plunged
their new warmth into a bucket and watched tiny bubbles
escape from the paralysed struggle. Two minutes expired.
They came out cold and bony. I put them in a sack
and threw it in the dam and watched it sink.
Today it floated to the surface.

Kite

I am plugged into the sky.
It is not pleased. A high, long,
windy sound coming down sharp string tells me
I am touching a nerve
on a loose connexion. I have to
readjust each time it hurts.
And though I have easily mesmerized
the sheep, the kite has done the same
to me. It pesters the sun like an insect
at a light. X-rays reveal two crossed bones.
A shadow swims around me in the flowing grass.
Mendicity has stiffened my arms and neck.
The kite is haggling over length. Its caprice has
burnt lines across my hands. I wait
for another tense struggle.
But not for long. The line is dead.
The kite has lost its nerve. A red rag
is kicking in the grass and I have won
a sudden disappointing victory.

The Dam

The dam at the end of the deep green field
is a metre of brown wrapping paper
covering the clay that hasn't congealed.
In the days before the excavator
two men with shovels dug it in a week.
When I was young I nearly drove the tractor
in. A load of fodder held us back.
In summer it's popular with the herd
who muck it up by floating green cow pats
and come out caked, with leeches on their teats.
In winter it's the spot for shooting birds.
Two ibises stand on the rim like taps.

The Wait

You write of what you know.

Waiting for test results.

It could go either way.

The room is filled with people
waiting for test results.

Somewhere else
the quality of light is different.
Late afternoon. Little men
playing cricket in football shorts.
Bodies glowing brown
like the dirt pitch. And miles away,
on the treeline, hundreds of cockatoos
breaking up the light.

That is nearly twenty years ago.
Your childhood.

It could be this time
or another.

Either way you write of death.
Your death.

It will be horrible. I know.

The Universal Pig

Some slow low shape slinks pink out of the blue.
Lazy but cunning it comes round the bend.
You think you see the pig before you do.

Something puts the wind up the kangaroo
Who bounds away to where the fences end.
Some slow low shape slinks pink out of the blue.

The dogs are raising hell at something new.
It will be more than they can comprehend.
You think you see the pig before you do.

Roosters are sounding cock-a-doodle-doo
As if the farmer's knife had been sharpened.
Some slow low shape slinks pink out of the blue.

In the dairy the cows are nervous too.
No gentle words can make the milk descend.
You think you see the pig before you do.

And in their pen the restless pigs look through
The rails for the arrival of their friend.
Some slow low shape slinks pink out of the blue.
Do you think you see the pig before you?

Country Football

The ellipse, Hindu symbol of fertility,
is flanked by crowded cars
nosing up to the rails.
It suckles like a sow.

Inside the cars voices report
from significant, never been there places –
Kardinia, Moorabbin, Windy Hill.

Reflecting each other from the cusps
rise two-dimensional white cathedrals.
Today they will be temples to apostasy twice.
Their entrances are guarded by clones
whose torches blaze pure white.

From corrugated iron purgatory
many men feed out in lines like parachutists,
limbs varnished with an intoxicating wake
of eucalyptus oil.

Landing near afflatus
they disperse into pairs
of cryptic numerical combinations.

But one without a number,
as resolutely white as the cue ball,
omnipotent in a classical pose,
holds aloft a red ellipse

and whistles up
a terrible trumpeting of car horns
for this afternoon's do or die.

Making Hay

In rectangular vertigo the balepress
gives prodigious birth.
From conception to delivery
takes less than a minute.
Humming down slow rows
of lucerne and paspalum it chews grass,
snakeskins, thistles, feathers, anything.
By midday it can do no more.
The paddock is a maze of compression
soon to be unravelled
by hay-carters starting at the edges.
Shirtless in cowskin chaps and gloves
they perform their complex dance
with eighty-pound bales
on an earthquaking load that shoves
a slackchained,
bouncing, banging, balesucking escalator
down bays of the marvellous smell
of cut grass.
When the dance is done,
easing to the monolith, they sit
with cigarettes on what they've made.
After the hay has been restacked
they take a big tyre tube
to the swimming hole and muddy the water
worse than cattle,
slushing after the slippery tube.
With one stye eye and sleek
black skin it is the nearest thing
to a leviathan in this billabong.

Question Time

In this country
the true test of imagination
is being able to name a paddock.

Think of Boiling Downs
where strips of fat are strung along the fence
and red and purple bits of gut
are lying round like broken toys.

How can you not then think of your own death?
(The one that made you kill those sheep.)
It's right through you,
efficiently out of control;
running down while always coming up with more,
aware that nothing can be done.
The prognosis says
you will die
in a paddock, which you have been thinking about
but which you have not seen.

No-one can say when.
It's a bit like flying standby
except they send a specialist who asks –
Do you grind your teeth at night?

Well, yes, sleeping scared, you do.
Going back over paddocks
more times than you did

as a child,
the nodal glands and nodal dreams
bring you awake
to another question –

What do you do with death?
It's nailing theses to the bedroom door.
You shout –

It's all right! I believe in death!
but the noise doesn't stop
sounding like the names of the dead
gathering names,
filling the telephone book with obituaries.

There are two things to say about this.
It has no consolation
and it means that what discoveries
there are left to make
will not involve the sense of touch.

Not like that time in the calving paddock
when you found a cart-wheel
woven down by grass.
You tore it free and rolled it home
not knowing you would have to write out
variations on –
Why was death announced so soon?

What you knew began with wonder
on your father's farm
and though it wouldn't be that good again
you could have gone on so easily.

Insomnia

The room is not spinning.
In darkness something the size of death
is just out of focus.
From other places of the house
well-worn little noises
colour the quiet stasis of fear.

Turning over I accept everything.
There is no going back
to the body's evanescent harmony.
Remission is not respite
and it's not worth crying out. Who
among the angelic orders would listen?

Rilke, you were written off
as one whose sickness was a mental thing.
With callous ignorance your doctors got it right.
The origins of this disease are in the mind,
and in your elegies.

The angels,
terrible in their German sensibilities,
are stacked and standing on the bookshelves.
Their shapes are more familiar now.
Fear has changed its colours
and from behind the slab of curtain
an outbreak of daylight is spreading.

Self-pity

Is not one of the seven deadly sins
although it gets more use since
that unsuspecting day when euphemisms
dropped their masks and the message was
WORDS CAN KILL.
Now the thought of never growing old
is with me all the time. I'm like the traveller
on the kerb in a strange city, gaping –
'My dreams!
I only put them down for a minute!'

Resting in the library was double-edged.
A close reading of the modernist big names
showed up themes of self-pity
and I, cheated by myself, could
write poems only in the first person singular –
This is serious and this is what it's like.
But happiness has been serendipity. It
happened in the ambulance on the way back
from celltrifuge. I sat up like a child
and smiled at dying young, at all
love's awfulness.

The Cause of Death

Suddenly I am waiting for slow death.
In the small hours I am groping towards
the kitchen worrying about the soft
collision, wondering when it will be.
I can hear the gum tree in the garden
creaking away like sex in the next room
and can see most of my life frame by frame
with the frightened sight of the condemned man.
Returning to an empty bed gone cold
it occurs to me that becoming one
in a hundred thousand has changed nothing
except what might have been another end.
The cause of death is in the blood and bone.
It breeds in the past, feeds on the future.

The Barbecue

The Sunday barbecue was hell.
Eye-stinging smoke and spitting fat
and flames almost out of control.
I didn't feel like eating meat,

not after having killed the sheep
two days ago, behind the shed,
and cut it mostly into chops
and seen my boots go dull with blood.

I served the fat-striated stuff
into a silver roasting dish
and settled down to have my lunch
(an omelette with tomato sauce)

and listened to a group of friends
who talked of anything but death.

A Difficult Calf

My father has always been reasonable.
I can remember him one cold Spring morning
losing a struggle with a big bony calf.
At first glance they both seemed to be
bending over, examining something
at the bottom of an old tin bucket.
But it wasn't curiosity in their concentration,
it was wilfulness.
My father had the calf by the head
and was pushing its face down into the whiteness,
unsuccessfully swearing at it to drink.
I thought the big-eyed thing would drown.
Whenever it managed to get its nose out
and make loud wet blowing sucking noises
the next time under would be longer.
I wasn't all that old
but I recognized the similarities
between the vaguely funny scene in front of me
and something I'd watched on the news
where two chunky American soldiers
were interrogating a Vietnamese peasant in a creek.
The bubbles especially were the same.
The news report was incomplete
but we were told the soldiers had gone too far.
Here though, with typical humanity,
my father couldn't be bothered going too far.
He straightened up, stepped back
and emptied the bucket of milk and hot water
all over the cause of his frustration.
I can remember him walking away
saying 'It can bloody well soak in!'
and the calf standing very still, dripping and steaming.

The Haystack

It wasn't just a pile of bales.
It was a home for baby possums,
dreamy kittens, disappearing snakes
and pertinacious willy-wagtails
I used to build a row of battlements
along the top and look out
from the castle's vantage point.
The view was at green symmetry
with barbed-wire seams,
and if the cows were near
the sound of all those mouths
rhythmically tearing the grass
would come clearly up.
We had a dog who more than once
came back from there
with bloody rips across his face
and something dead and furry
in his mouth. But only once
I found him dead up there.
One long hot afternoon I left
my mother in the kitchen baking bread
and went outside to see a massive loaf
sun-crusted and fresh inside.
Later on it became a testing place
for cigarettes and cans of beer
and then when I no longer had to hide
those things I had to learn the way
the stack was made. That took a while.
My first attempt collapsed
within a few days of the event
but what we found could just as well
have been there for a thousand years.
The bay was open like a quarry
and a company of rough stone blocks
that would have made a temple for the king

was left abandoned on the ground.
It seemed the empire had collapsed.
One season after that the stack
burnt down. It went up at sunset.
The first we knew of it was when
the neighbours drove around *en masse*
as if they had been waiting for a signal.
The sun went down obscured by smoke
and in the morning everything was black.
We never should have pressed those bales so green.
In the following phoenix weeks
I was impressed by how
insurance money and contract lucerne
could resurrect a stack so quickly.
The smoke had hardly cleared
before we saw again the pristine mass
of one of Proust's metonymic cathedrals.
When I think how many times
the haystack's meaning changed
I also think how much
its purpose stayed the same.
There must have been a moral
there for love and hungry cows
because no matter what the weather
we were always giving it away.

The Needle

You come and go
at an angle

sometimes giving
sometimes taking

Your calling card
is sealed with red

(or purple
if you're nervous)

There is always
a cover-up

after you've gone
(you go without air)

You have a sharp
nose for blood

and a head
full of drugs

You have
your favourite spots

and you work alone

The Change

I ride along the Yabba track
before the day gets really hot,
and wonder what it will be like
when chronic changes to acute.

The biography said Rilke had
four weeks of pure, relentless pain.
I think he would have found his God
about as useless as morphine.

There's so much space at Yabba North
it's hard to think an early death
could toss a rider off his horse
and leave him trampled underneath.

And yet the change will surely come –
as sure as I am riding home.

The Pressure

One afternoon I dreamt of what I've got
as being an outsize feral animal.
I was at the end,
caught up terribly in a boundary fence,
been there for days, no-one around
except some wide-winged, plangent birds
whirlpooling way above me
and the animal,
which had been hanging about all afternoon,
staring, working closer.
When it got to me the wires shook
and thoughts of release were swallowed whole.
I tried to push it off
but it wrapped strong jaws
around my good right arm
and squeezed and squeezed until I woke.

The nurse was there, taking my blood pressure.
The tubing round my arm was tight
and what she pumped it with,
in the palm of her hand,
was black and oval-shaped
like a spider's abdomen.

Death Who

The conversation with cancer
begins equitably enough.
You and he are summing each other up,
trading ripostes and *bons mots*
before the soup.
Everything seems ordinary.
There is interest and boredom,
and you've been drinking all afternoon,
which could mean that you're depressed
or that you're in good form.
You get each other's measure
and the conversation settles,
subjects divide and increase like cells.
Gradually you realize
that like the background Mozart
all the emotions are involved,
and that you're no longer saying as much.
Put it down to strength of intent.
He's getting aggressive
and you're getting tired. Someone
says he's a conversational bully
but you're fascinated.
He tells you things about yourself,
forgotten things and those not yet found out,
pieces from childhood and the unhealing wound.
It's all there.
Forgetting food, you drink. (Too much
red wine will encourage nightmares
but that's not a problem now.) – You marvel.
Isn't he tireless!
A raconteur like something out of Proust.
He blows cigar smoke into your face
and makes a little joke.
It's actually too much.
You're tired and the more you tire

the more the words are everywhere.
You go and recline on the couch,
but he won't shut up. He follows you there
and makes the cushions uncomfortable for you.
It's so unjust.
Your host is in the kitchen,
all the guests have gone
and cancer's got you like conviction
and he's kneeling on your chest,
glaring over you,
pushing a cushion into your face,
talking quietly and automatically,
the words not clear.
He's got you and he's really pushing,
pushing you to death.

The Birds

The time is nearly five a.m.
and all the birds are on the go.
They sound just like the frequencies
of many twiddled radios.

It's really bad the way it's gone –
I always used to sleep okay
and dream and miss the rural life
and never see the break of day.

But since I got the only part
in cancer's scripted dialogue
I've heard those birds a million times
and seen the sun come up a lot.

I've been rehearsing death each night,
and still I haven't got it right.

Spleen

Lousy little spleen
nestling in your basket of ribs

Unbalancer of my blood
and purse of spent white cells

I prayed for you
without result

* * *

Unhappy spleen
small wonder

folk wisdom nominated you
the seat of melancholy

Others said you were
the source of merriment
but Baudelaire

saw pain's black flag
planted on my skull

* * *

Nasty little spleen
you'll swell up like a football
when mad leukaemia's
on the march again

Today
the doctors pressed their cold fingers
up under my ribs
to get to you

Do you remember
years ago
how I would reach up under the culvert
to tickle out trout

or redfin,
how I was
tensed for the inevitability of yabbies?

* * *

Abysmal little spleen
you're as elusive as
a fish

You kept me up all night looking
for a voice
to condemn you in

What use was that?

You only listen to chemotherapy
You listen and then you don't

From here the paradigm
is mystery
You weren't the cause –
though you knew all along

Walking Through the Crop

It doesn't matter any more
the way the wheat is shivering
on such a beautiful hot day
late in the afternoon, in Spring.

I couldn't care about the sound
of insects frying in the heat
or how a flock of cockatoos
has one up in a brilliant sheet.

I had a list I tried to keep.
Sometimes I even wrote it down.
It had all sorts of private things
like images, sensations, sounds...

There's nothing in these dying days.
I've given everything away.

Planting Them

for the West Melbourne Potato Appreciation Society

This soil looks almost good enough to eat
and smells just like a loaf of wholemeal bread.
You know that here potatoes should do well
because the ground is mad with nettle shoots.

We get to work with bucketfuls of dull
pink nuggets, dropping them in crooked rows.
You could do worse than see the winter out
with nothing but a sack of pontiacs.

There's half an acre's worth of rows to plant.
The afternoon moves down to tractor pace
and quiet talk gives way to tractor noise
as each of us is humbled by our work.

Tonight we'll go up to the lamp-lit house
and bake potatoes in the open fire.

A Bit of Bitterness

It is waking,
not having forgotten that you have leukaemia,
that no-one is watching over you.
In such darkness
the luminous numbers three one nine
don't mean a thing.
There is only faithlessness.
You envy others their belief in God
and do not understand
how death cannot be irreplaceable.
A year ago in hospital
you saw your friends much differently.
Their faces were a long way off.
Remembering that time
you mouth the platitudes they said to you,
the platitudes they heard from you,
and feel left out.
They came to see themselves,
and you, the already dead, could not intrude.
Your bit-part is to play
composure in uncertainty, and later,
dignity in long pain.
But fear has seen through this act of being
philosophical about death
and it has made you believe bitter things
about your friends.
Their faces are too many and too close.

The numbers change and change.

You will not sleep again tonight.

Ich Bin Allein

'Cancer is a rare and still scandalous
subject for poetry; and it seems
unimaginable to aestheticize the disease.'
Susan Sontag, Illness as Metaphor

It is in every part. Nothing can be cut off or out.
A steady suddenness.
It isn't Keats
or randomness.
It is this body
nurturing its own determined death.
I will find out how much pain is in this body
and I will not behave myself.
It isn't fit for poetry
but since
poets create their own mythology
there is no choice.
My friends have all gone home.
I'm in the dank half-light. I am alone.

The Guest

In April, after leaving hospital,
I went to stay with friends out in the sticks.
That day I walked for hours along the creek

and saw the spoonbills wait, then push their white
into a see-through sky. And though I knew
that everything had come unstuck, it made

no sense. At dinner-time I talked about
the steady changes in the cancer cells
and how I only had three years to live

and how an early death will concentrate
the mind. But their first child, just ten weeks old,
kept interrupting what I said. He had

an appetite for mother's milk and more.
He didn't care about my table talk
or how I hadn't touched my solid food.

His unformed words were full of sense. This death
is new to me as noticing the space
between a waxing and a waning life.

I bedded in the room where that child slept
and when I woke up somewhere in the night
it wasn't for those perfect hungry cries.

Dead Calf

I went out in the first light
to where the dark Friesian was.
She seemed resigned to a head at either end.
It was too early for flies.
I noosed the smaller head
and leaned back with the rope.
A dead calf crashed onto the ground.
Its eyes were clear
and its little tongue was sticking out.
Its mother started eating the afterbirth.
She must have been damaged inside.
As I walked away
something spilled out like applause.

Trip Cancelled

It's happened as they said it would.
While I was shoring up my hopes
and making plans to go abroad
remission has discreetly stopped.

Last night I tentatively pinned
a map of Europe on my wall
and dreamt its cities of the mind –
those languages, that sense of scale.

Today the doctor spoke of death
but what I thought of was a day
back on the dappled farm beneath
the peppertree a life ago.

The words for death are all too clear.
I write the poem dumb with fear.

Apologies

I'm sorry.
Because it's only possible
to think in clichés
when the end is really nigh
there won't be any standing back
to write like no-one else.
Because it's really happening. The symptoms
wouldn't lie. The bruising,
bleeding, swelling, loss of sight:
I'll hate this death
because it gives the meaning back
to words I never thought I'd have to use.
I can't explain. The words
are plain, the images obvious –
'This was the last work. Notice the crows.'

That's the way the symptoms really are –
not the body sending first calls now
and last calls now
but two married people
sitting in a hospital corridor
gazing down the length of sorrow.
Their only child will not bury them.
I must tell them how sorry I am.

The Shoot

The rabbit shoot was bags of fun.
We came across them by surprise
and let them have it on the run.
The one I got was still alive

until I cracked him with the butt.
I pulled his skin off like a sock
and then I emptied out his guts
and stuffed him in my little sack.

The trouble is this isn't true.
I made it up because I'm bored
of being alone up here with you
in Ward 10 West, the cancer ward.

It has no bearing on the truth.
It's just a vehicle for death.

From County Down

Crows. Maybe a hundred.
And up there the nests. A cluster
of crow-bombs in the bare beech trees.
No other birds around here
have it so willingly tough. We watch one homing,
heavy with a mouthful of the spartan sticks.
My uncle has a mountain and a hill
and can remember them free of crows. Now
flying shadows are his heaviness
and you won't get him to destroy the nests
because it brings bad luck.
Instead, he will walk across steep fields in March
and see again,
the red wet triangles under eyes no longer there,
what crows will do to lambs.

Coming to the wintry trees
I choose a metaphor. The nests
are black clots in my map
of arteries and veins. But on the skyline
nothing is bleaker than straight talking
so I head off in that direction,
forgetting the name of the famous footballer –
diagnosed on Tuesday, dead on Thursday.
Crows always make you think of mortality.
Even as I walk they are ruining
this landscape. Those swans
are bits of rubbish on the lake

and I will not be suffering a late death.
My bad luck is to write the same poem every time.
A sort of postcard poem
from the rookery. *Timor mortis conturbat me.*
I never wanted this.

Resurrection

In hospital my varied worlds
finished up in one small room.
Faces resurrected from years ago
and days ago looked round at faces
or looked at me.
They weren't sure
what they were doing there
but I had a clue. Five letters.
The opposite of life.
It made me want to throw my words
around the room
but I never did.
Voices held me back, saying –
I must be moderate, for my friends.
Now I'm coming good again
like those euphoric souls
who don't believe that death
has come to them in public hospitals,
the only visitor that day.
I see myself
resurrected from time to time
in the conversations of people I knew.
They're talking about the way I died.
A sort of tragedy for some
though not for me
because the scenes would only happen once.
If anything is tragic in these unrepeated days
it's this –
I don't know what I've lost.
The possibilities are over there
among the things that need belief.
And what is here is unbelievable
and hard to explain.
For instance –
These are my physical thoughts,

and this is my undrinkable blood.
The thoughts are not my own
and the blood is making me write
letters in verse.
I like the way the letters
might be read by anyone later on.
I half believe that it's another way
of coming back.

An Education

At first there was a dairy farm
with subjects coming from the soil –
a grid of paddocks big with time,
about a hundred cows, one bull.

Regrettably it didn't last.
The subjects got more difficult.
I studied Love but didn't pass
and gave up God with no result.

I couldn't think what else there was
until I went up to a ward
where people died, and met a face
that gently told me what I had.

The final subject has been set.
I'm concentrating hard on Death.

Hotel Minerva

The trains push out of Ravenna Central
like abacus lines, and the alsatian
cruising the unlit yard three floors down
is an aquarium shark who can't see how
two small cakes of soap have just hit him.
And across the curved mosaic water
an ornithoid steel crane waits to adjust
industry's thin skyline in the morning.
There's nothing else here that I want to see.
The hotel receptionist doesn't know
that I've got an unbelievable disease,
that I don't have to write travel poems.
Nor does anyone else in this country,
and telling strangers never works out right.
I've discovered that it isn't so good
to try to make each day significant.
The unfamiliar makes me think of home.
I don't care about Early Christian art
or bits of poets' bones in marble huts
because contracting this serious disease
gave me a subject on a mirrored plate
but didn't give me time to find the words
even though they're short, familiar ones.

Sant'Ivo della Sapienza

No square pegs or round holes here
everything goes.
The corners of the hexagon
are jutting like reversed wings
of fighter planes from the next century
but they go back in design
to Hadrian's *Teatro Marittimo*
while the ground plan goes shrinkingly
up to the top of the dome.
Somewhere in between there's space
so thick and unified it's rabbit-proof.
Such an organism makes me think of flowers
and bees, or in the dark a cog.
Either way, as autonomy it changes to the carapace
where, without a change of style,
a Babel ziggurat is drilling Eastern air
and pyrotechnics are really conch.
On top of that, like its human counterpart,
the cross on dove on globe on cage miracle
is a balancing trick prolonged by believing.
But, disappointingly, even here
death has got past the caretaker
to discredit Borromini's biographies.
This delicate unity is an acceptance
whose membrane needs another coat of white.
In the final composition
all eyes are turned up
and the ribs are showing through.
Is this the dilatation of wisdom
or is it the fabulous triple echo?

Radio Thanatos

I heard a documentary on the radio
about the act of death.
It said that hearing is the final sense to die.
'Our last experience is through the ears'
reminded me of how my premonitions
and disbeliefs were aural too.
It seemed to me
that I was driving in from the back country
over a rough road,
the long aerial waving in waves.
Increasingly I heard
the sheen of city radio with fewer cracks.
It began wistfully, almost unconsciously,
like Satie's *gymnopédies*.
Some of the songs got lost in memory
until the heavy metal shaking
of the hospital bed,
then after treatment a somewhere radio
played sixties drug music all weekend.
They told me this had been a program change –
there wasn't any time to run the scheduled shows.
I can't predict the closing down
but would expect
the atonal miscellany of hospital sounds.

Bad News

And even if there is a remission
there is always a follow-up letter
saying the cancer has started again,
cancelling what the previous letter said.
After that second envelope arrived
from Rome I carried it round for three days
before gutting it in a Fitzroy pub.
I was drinking Guinness by the handful,
dark as blood pudding and nearly as thick.
The alcohol was ineluctable.
It spread along my arteries and veins
the way the word went through my list of friends
when I was sent up to the cancer ward.
And yes of course, the letter was bad news.
I've had no solace knowing someone else
who has this thing. We know what will happen,
and how it uses pain as a motif:
the other times disappearing like friends.
There's only one more letter to receive.
Perhaps it has already been dispatched.

From *Down the Lake with Half a Chook*

Death After Life

We shared a cygnet by the lake,
and heading back from there on foot
the spent syringes sounded like
the autumn leaves beneath my feet.

The hospital was full of folks
who'd lost their appetite and hair,
and when the doctor got up close
he stank of cigarettes and beer.

Tonight you turned the telly on
and told me cancer's not as bad
as watching telly on your own.
I washed the chemo down with red

and thought about the opening line,
how death was not a problem then.

The Drip

Woke up this morning
to find the needle
torn out of my arm
although the small pain
was still in there.
I've only got myself
to blame. A wrong move
in the busy night.
There's a clear stain
on the sheet
where the drip
had a wet dream.
And there's a bit of blood
in certain places
on the sheet
and on the hospital pyjamas.
The tape and gauze
across my inside arm
are lying there
like dirty clouds,
and what is underneath
is like a gorgeous sunrise.
If I could turn
to look outside
would I see metaphors
of this?
I see the needle
on the floor.
A silver twig
in a chemical pond.
I never liked it much.
The night they pushed it in,
this four-inch nail,
they touched
a metaphoric nerve.

I squirmed.
My heart was hammering
in its cage.
The needle ached immediately
and then the sedative,
and everything
slowed down.
I noticed no-one else in here
was so upset
about their drip,
and that the nurses
always came to see
not me but it.
I came around.
The drip went everywhere
with me
like thoughts
of what had happened.
If I went down the corridor
to have a shower
it followed me.
Its shiny bones
would jangle
like the trailer's steel
when we were feeding out
on healthy mornings
years ago.
In the shower
I'd hold my arm up
in a plastic bag
as if the drip
were giving me an oath.
At night
the drip stood over me
and fed my dreams.
I dreamed
about its scarecrow frame,

an inside aerial
that only gets one show.
It touched me
with its silver finger
and left a poisoned splinter
in my arm
as the coastline drifted
out of sight.
The sea was very warm
and then the rubber boat
got punctured
by a swordfish
from the deep.
A single-masted ship
threw out a line
but when I woke
the line was out of reach.
That was half an hour ago.
In thirty minutes more
the morning shift begins.
The light is fully here.
I reach and
PUSH FOR NURSE

The Secret

They call this country marginal.
My plans for growing crops have all
turned out to be impossible –
there's something lacking in the soil.

There's not much hay to feed the cows,
and all the eucalyptus trees
around the never-finished house
have got a terminal disease.

It's been a while since I received
a visit from my many friends
or even from the nursing aid
who always says I'm on the mend.

I'm living out here on the sly.
There must be better ways to die.

Leeches

Swim like sunken ripples.
Bloody-minded
they come home
to what they know –
the single fact of blood.
Who could singe them off
with cigarettes
for that?
They'd prefer you not to know
they're there.

From Ward 10 West
(with this presence
leeching trusted lifetime)
I can see them in the channel still.
They cling to my imagination
in soft black lines of thought
even though
the use of them in hospitals
has fallen off.
Yes. They hang like bits of gut,
then drink up big
and swell like sails.

Receiving concentrated blood
from a plastic bag
as plump as a happy leech
I follow a line back
to duck shooters
standing in the swamp
with shotguns
flat against their chests
like windmills windless.
When they walked out
in shorts
their legs were covered

in a sleek black down of leeches.
On this they threw salt
and the darkness fell away.

In summer
cows were just the same.
A cow that came to milking
from a channel
or a dam
would never be alone.
Washing round the udder's bulk
I'd pull down
puffy sacs of blood,
splat them
on the milkwet concrete
and stirring it
with my toe
produce a lovely milkshake pink.

More recently
they've helped me get a metaphor.
I picked off one
about leukaemia being a leech
because it wants your blood
before you know what's happened,
and because the sucking leech
gets big and ugly
like the final stages
of the cancer cell.
And though this
sticking words like leeches
to the page
will make no difference
to what the cancer knows or does,
I had to tell you anyway.
The soft uncertainties
are gathering
round the smell of blood,
coming home to what they know.

The Effect

What a surprise to be living
entirely in the present. As late as yesterday
you wouldn't have thought it were possible
but sometime in the night
they took away the old bloke over there,
the one with lung cancer. He'd been cough
non-stop like a loose sheet of roofing iron
in the wind. It grated on us all.
One of the others said to him, 'Listen mate
if you're gonna die will you do it quietly'
but he didn't seem to hear.
Anyway things are wonderful now,
so peaceful. Here comes the nurse
with her drug trolley rattling
like one of those portable cocktail bars.
She tells me she doesn't like whingers
and gives me more morphine,
a double dose, injected directly into my sidekick
the drip. The effect is delectable –
so smooth, smooth as whisky.
It gets me first down the back of the legs
like sliding into some long warm bath.
Maybe death is this easy, maybe I've had it
wrong all the time. Too tense.
They say you should be relaxed when you fall.

The Deadline

has passed. Three years spoken for
by a specialist doing his job
a shade over three years ago.
What he gave me was a mean figure
taken from the dead like sheets
and the words he used to do it
are still special tonight in this old house.
Everyone else has closed their eyes
to the problem of darkness
but that simple explanation of the deadline
is keeping me on this side of sleep
so I come out of the bedroom
and turn on the kitchen light.
There's a spider passing across the table.
One of those delicate ones
with a body the size of a teardrop
and thin clear legs arching
in eight directions like a miniature fountain.
At the moment before I press
the spider into the table
I remember what that Italian girl
who didn't have long to live
told me about not killing them.
She said they're good luck in Calabria
and let me hear the name
they have for them over there –
a word that escapes me now
except that it was beautiful.
There's no getting away from the fact
that sentimentality won't make it reappear
so I go back to bed,
to the problem of darkness.

Pudge

I don't know what it was about the two
of us. We just didn't hit it off.
Eventually we had this vicious blue
outside the dining room and he lost.

After that I thought he'd given up.
We'd pass each other in the corridor
without a look or anything and at
the Easter break he shifted to another dorm.

One afternoon in second term I chased
a ball behind the gym when just like that
something yellow went whizzing past my face.
What could have made a whizzing noise like that?

I went to where it landed in the shade
and found an apple stuck with razor blades.

The Cow

The group of boys
moves slowly down the channel,
more slowly than a cow would walk.
The sky has little depth
and they have unreflecting health
with more of it ahead of them.
Their mode of transport is a bloated cow
that submarines each time they all get on.
In paddocks to the left and right of them
the simple clover grows.
Not long ago the cow was eating it,
aware of nothing but the luscious taste
and gassy aftertaste.
She's never been as far from home as this –
two miles from Wilson's bend
where Wilson and his children
dragged her in.
When she had gone the other cows
kept coming back to sniff the place
and take off all at once
as if they had the wind up about something.
And now the boys have found her out like flies.
They cling to her while leeches cling to them.
They row the legs as stiff as oars
and break the tail
and look into the eyes as dull as mud.
One boy will think of days like this
more often than the rest.
At milking time the group will separate
and she, the cow,
will gradually drift apart.

Strathbogie Ranges 1965

We left the car just off the track
and wandered up towards the view.
It would have been about three o'clock.
The sky was Nunawading Blue.

A little way before the end
we stopped. Stretched right across the track
like something out of Disneyland
was this enormous carpet snake.

He was flicking his tongue at us
as if he couldn't keep it still.
We couldn't help but notice –
the tongue was something else's tail.

A Farm in the High Country

We visited that farm in the high country
after driving for hours on slow mountain tracks
that wound like intestines through sturdy forest
and made a backseat child sick in the guts.
Everything about the place was over the hill.
The old farmer was bent small like a snow gum
and his border collie lay in a flower bed
ashamed of the bare scabby patches down his back
that were the same as the great bare patches
up on the ridges where the loggers had been.
It was easy to mistake the noise of their semis
grinding through the trees somewhere over there
for the noise of the sawmill at Mittagundi.
And it was easy not to notice that black snake
sunning itself on top of some worn-out tyres
until it melted off quickly like boiling rubber
and flowed through a stretch of dry grass
with the sound of the grass beginning to burn.
Behind the shed was a jumble of rusty carcasses –
implements that must have been there for years
now being pulled under by long tenacious grass.
A horse-drawn baler with its fat bottom lip,
a stump-jump plough with its wheels missing,
dozens of other things broken beyond recognition.
They looked helpless and ridiculous – and yet
at one time they had been essential to the farm.
We must have arrived there at milking time
because the cows were crowded up to their gate
like housewives before the start of a big sale.
Looking at their old black-and-white Friesian bull
was like looking beyond him to the shapes
of half-melted snow on the rump of Mount Bogong.
From his small yard he stared back enormously
in an almost convincing display of menace – and yet

there was something in it that couldn't help but show
a life numbed by enclosure, something as ruinous
and indifferent as the skyline that surrounded us.

The Devil's Work

With a cattle prod
he steers her away from the others
and into the crush,
shoulders the gate up hard behind her
and bolts it.

She shits immediately
but can't lift her tail enough.
It slides down her back legs
or monkey-like
drops down the bars of the steaming gate.
It's only grass.

At the other end
he pulls across a length of pipe
that keeps her head in place.
She jerks back in alarm.
Ears become blinkers
and mucus trails from her nose like afterbirth.
It's only water.

With his fingers
he pincers the rubbery slimy nose
and forces her head up.
Into the open mouth
he slots a drenching-gun and squeezes out
the milky stuff.
It goes down noisily.

Next, with an enormous pair of boltcutters
and a crackle like firewood
he takes off one of the horns
and then the other.
Thin lines spray shadows
on her face and on the concrete.
It's only blood.

With something like an electric soldering-iron
he singes the wounds against rain.
It hurts like the devil
and makes a burnt obsessive smell.

He knows that for weeks ahead
the cows won't go near
this part of the yard
no matter how many times it's hosed down.
If herded up to it
they will baulk
and stare at something terrible.

When he lets the drenched hornless cow
out of the crush
it wanders down the lane
to a paddock with an open gate.

He does all this again and again
gradually diminishing the size of the herd
and the day.

He does it so many times
that his thoughts become unfocused and move
slowly, without much purpose,
like cows in a paddock.

If pressed for details now
he couldn't help
though everything about it is clear to me.
I was there, nine years old,
sitting on the fence.

Sludge

What is it about the past?
We're always trying to go back there,
turning off the bitumen near Merv's place
and heading down that last mile and a half of gravel
for no other reason than to show
a new friend the old farm
and all those places that look so small now.
They don't matter to anyone else
and yet here we are
pointing out the spot under the sugar gum
where a nine-year-old boy
stood in quiet surprise one afternoon
and watched a goanna shake herself out of the earth
having laid her eggs
down in the warmth of a termite nest.
And looking over at the weatherboard house
other details start coming back to us –
how there were always possums in the roof
and the way they made terrible noises at night
not unlike a cappuccino machine
and that their fights would go on for ages
and circle like a storm above us.
We remember lying in our bedroom
a hole the size of a fist in the ceiling
where a small pink tentative nose
would sometimes be lowered and then withdrawn
and that one of the neighbours
had lost his false teeth one night
from the glass of water beside his bed
and they weren't found
until he went into the roof a few months later
to check some wiring
and there they were
lying in the dust like part of a fossil.
We can't help remembering

the time we cleaned out the rainwater tank
and found a possum skeleton in the sludge.
It comes back to us now after a long time
and we try to explain it to people
who weren't there –
the way that perfect little frame
was curled in fine mud
and how clean it was, the flesh all gone.
But it's of no interest to them.
They merely smile at us like indulgent parents
as we drive back towards the present
down smooth roads that become less familiar
the closer the city gets
and we arrive there with nothing to say
exhilarated by the mundane.

The Drop Kick

Extinct in the big league
because the extra time it takes
can get you unloaded
the drop kick is still alive
on a country ground
if the weather's right.
To shoot for goal with one
the way Jack Savage used to do
is a sign of confidence.
He could do it easily
from centre half-forward
and the story goes he did it once
from out on the wing.
His greatest moment
was winning the '59 Grand Final with one –
a running roost in time-on.
It was poetry all the way –
seventy yards and spinning like a boomerang.
Not bad for a thirty-four-year-old
who played the second half
with a broken rib.
Today, from the noise and warmth
of the J.W. Savage Stand
the drop kick looks a piece of cake
to these half-pissed farmers' sons.
They're going to take the field
at half time in a ritual display.
Will anyone tell them the risk?
It's usually embarrassment –
a grubber off the side of the boot.
But sometimes it's worse.

Dirt Roads

The good thing about dirt roads is the way
they change.
You might be driving along
a smooth powdery stretch
beside a paddock where the farmer
is turning his windrows of hay
and the terracotta dust
will be pumping out the back of the car
in a huge row that turns slowly
as it rises into the still afternoon air
when suddenly the road goes gravelly
and there is the sound of a quarrel
beneath you.
Most of it is muffled and deep-throated
but there is also a top register
of small sharp stones
pinging off the metal as they shoot up.
You don't get this variety with a sealed surface.
Bitumen is monoculture
whereas half an hour on a dirt road
can be like Mozart's 'Fantasy in D Minor' –
it can have all of life in it.
And unlike the indifference of bitumen
dirt roads keep a transitory record
for the interest of anyone on foot
i.e. the fluent script where a snake flowed across
or the continuous tangled lines
of a pushbike going home.
A sealed road might be more consistent
but a dirt one is more eventful.
What you lose in droning regularity
you make up for in fun.
First time I drove across the Nullarbor
it wasn't sealed
and a lot of it was badly corrugated.

There were three of us
in a souped-up old Valiant.
We found the faster you went
the better it was. At eighty
you floated deafeningly over
the crumpled road
and everything on the dash shivered off.
It was like the beginning
of a private earthquake.
The suspension had a nervous breakdown
and we laughed all the way.
Next day in Perth we treated Val
to a new set of red shockers
and she felt a lot firmer.
Things like that don't seem to happen much
any more. Whenever they seal a dirt road
they make it deadly boring
especially at night.
On long straight sections anywhere round Australia
night-drivers get tired at the monotony
and occasionally one of them goes to sleep
and rolls over violently
or drifts into a badly shaken tree.
The fact that it was a smooth ride to death
is no consolation.
They ought to stop covering the country
with these high-speed conveyor belts.
Nobody looks happy driving along them.
And where are they all going anyway?

The Drum Net

I made the drum net out of chicken wire
and baited it with a bright red bottle top
(that's the colour they really go for)
and chucked it in down near the swamp.

I knew it wasn't legal to use a drum net
but that didn't matter much round here.
The bailiffs had better things to think about
than this sort of stuff. They didn't care.

I reefed it out a while later and found
some sad wreckage. One of the shags
had dived in there, got stuck and drowned.
Its wings were all twisted out of shape.

I walked slowly back across the paddock
where my father had spread hay for the cows.
It was sundown, and in the spreading shadows
the hay reminded me of drifts of snow.

Chopped Prose with Pigs

There was one old barrel-size boar
who just couldn't hold off
until the gate had been dragged open.
On that evening, after milking,
when we reversed down the lane
with a load of reject peaches from the cannery
this pig charged the electric fence
like some quixotic warrior whose time
had come. Knowing what the wires held
he started screaming with metallic vigour
way back before he got to the pain.
We stood on the trailer in filthy stasis
like two ham actors
upstaged by a member of the audience.
When it arrived the moment
was wonderful. The scream
went up to an ecstasy and the pig,
soaking with mud, hurled and dragged
itself frighteningly under the wires
while at the arch of contact
blue sparks burned into the twilight
and into my memory.
I had never seen so much intensity
for so many small peaches.

But pigs will eat other things as well,
including their offspring, and you.
There was a farmer up at Yabba North
who came unstuck in a pen
full of pigshit and duplicitous saddlebacks
one ordinary morning in January.
When they hosed out the place
they found about half the things
he had been wearing
plus all the bigger bones.

I saw his widow doing some shopping in town
not long after the funeral.
She was loaded down with supermarket bags
and grief.

Another time we found a bloated cow
tipped over in a far paddock.
The dead-cow truck wasn't coming round
so my father tied her to the tractor
and lurched her down the lane
like a small ship in a gentle swell.
We stopped in the smell of pigs
and while I rolled a cigarette
he broke her into half a dozen pieces
with an axe
and threw them over to the pigs.
When I went back early the next day
I stood rolling another cigarette
and looked at all the bigger bones
and the pigs lying round in the innocent mud.

It was one of those same pigs, a sow,
who got out of the churned-up paddock
and went down to the dairy one afternoon.
In the passageway there was a cattledog tied up
to keep cats out of the milkroom,
but he didn't worry about the pig.
She got in there
and tipped over an eight-gallon cream can
and then licked it all up.
We found her three days later
lying very still in an empty drain
with a relentless cream hangover.
Her eyes were so bloodshot
that whenever she opened them
it looked like she would bleed to death.

She recovered
but later on she did go out that way.
It happened early in the spring.
I coaxed her into a single pen mechanically
and smashed her between the eyes
with a hammer.
After pushing a knife through the jugular
I rolled her to one side
until most of the blood had pumped out.
It spread across the concrete
like an accident
and made me think how the cream
must have spread the same way.
I scalded and scoured her thoroughly
and when I hung her up
and drew the knife down her front
some of the guts pushed out
like odds and sods from an overloaded cupboard.
Reaching in for the rest
had me disgorging handfuls of animal warmth.

When the job was done
I hoisted her out of catreach
in muslin as clean as a bridal veil
and threw the chopped shinbones
to the cattledog.
I can still hear him
outside his tipped-over forty-four
chewing them with a sloppy broken rhythm.

The Noise

We pulled down the old chook yard
because it was too near the house.
It attracted the mice and they always
seemed to finish up over with us.

They'd be there unexpectedly
when you opened your eyes during grace
or sometimes at breakfast you'd discover
dark pellets mixed in with the flakes.

So we put up a new yard down near
the dairy and I fashioned a crow trap
out of some wire that was left over
and tossed in the remains of a sheep.

It worked like a charm. By the end
of the day there were dozens of crows.
I slithered inside and beat them to death
with a stick. Imagine the noise.

Shooting the Dogs

There wasn't much else we could do
that final day on the farm.
We couldn't take them with us into town,
no-one round the district needed them
and the new people had their own.
It was one of those things.

You sometimes hear of dogs
who know they're about to be put down
and who look up along the barrel of the rifle
into responsible eyes that never forget
that look and so on,
but our dogs didn't seem to have a clue.

They only stopped for a short while
to look at the Bedford stacked with furniture
not hay
and then cleared off towards the swamp,
plunging through the thick paspalum
noses up, like speedboats.

They weren't without their faults.
The young one liked to terrorize the chooks
and eat the eggs.
Whenever he started doing this
we'd let him have an egg full of chilli paste
and then the chooks would get some peace.

The old one's weakness was rolling in dead sheep.
Sometimes after this he'd sit outside
the kitchen window at dinner time.
The stink would hit us all at once
and we'd grimace like the young dog
discovering what was in the egg.

But basically they were pretty good.
They worked well and added life to the place.

I called them back enthusiastically
and got the old one as he bounded up
and then the young one as he shot off
for his life.

I buried them behind the tool shed.
It was one of the last things I did before
we left.
Each time the gravel slid off the shovel
it sounded like something
trying to hang on by its nails.

Going Back for a Look

The places round the billabong
are pretty much the way they were
but like a lot of things, they're gone.

It's strange to drive for hours alone
then turn the engine off and stare
at places round the billabong.

They look the same but they belong
to other people now. That's where
they're like a lot of things, they're gone.

I often used to walk along
the rabbit tracks and check my snares
at places round the billabong.

But now they keep the rabbits down
with bait. It's good to come this far
and find a lot of things have gone,

that all the snares have been undone
and what I wanted isn't here.
These places round the billabong
are like a lot of things, they're gone.

The Past

Watering the paddocks is what it's all about.
They've set up a whole network of channels, drains,
culverts and checkbanks to do it. The farmer
knows that right through summer, say every
fortnight, he's got to keep his paddocks irrigated
without using up his water allowance. Some summers
it's not easy. A couple of years back the change
was later than anyone could remember and no-one
made it. They had spotter planes flying over
the district to check for stolen water in shining
paddocks. And that same year they ringbarked all
the trees along the channel banks to save water.

* * *

This morning, a bit after eleven, the farmer
(with his son trying to keep up behind him)
strode over to the north-east corner of the farm
and heaved up the iron sluicegate. A sudden weight
of channel water heaved in irresistibly like strong
memory and shoved the big black wheel behind him
into slow turns that mean money. Some of the water
crashed up into his gumboots and almost immediately
his son (having caught up with him) started
running away beside the straight banks. He was
fascinated by the long tongue of water thrusting
down the dry mouth of the drain as fast as he
could go. For probably half a mile he ran parallel
to it with the same urgency and interest that
later on would make him want to write it down.

* * *

If you stayed around for the next few days
you'd see the farmer out walking along a drain bank,
stopping at certain places to dig a gap
there and let the water spread like faith
into that part of the paddock. And you'd see

82

his son running through the warm flood
in footy shorts, maybe stopping to look at a fish
(redfin or spotted trout) that somehow found itself
gliding over summer pasture after the violence
of magnetic entry and a rush down the drain.
And after that, when the sluicegate guillotined
the headwaters and the drains began to drain,
there'd be shags and kingfishers hanging round
the culvert pools hoping for a feed. And the farmer's
son would be there too, down on his hands and knees,
reaching in for something as elusive as the day
it happened.

From *Animal Warmth*

Pregnant Cow

Her swollen belly was a hammock,
somewhere to sleep, a nice warm bath.
This morning in the foggy paddock
I found some mushrooms, and a calf.

Milk

It's no good any more.
They've treated every last bucketful
so it always tastes the same,
so it never separates
and so it rots instead of souring.
My father used to say
'Homogenized, pasteurized and buggerized.'
And he was right.
They've ruined milk
just to kill a few bacteria
that the bureaucrats couldn't swallow.
And worse than that the ritual's gone.
There's no more going out at first light
to move a hundred drowsy cows
from the warm flattened places
they've created overnight;
to walk them
in the same sequence every time
down the lane,
so many hard feet on gravel
the sound of a slow landslide;
and to push them easily into the bails
and strip heavy udders,
the cats coming on time
through the forest of legs
to lick milk off concrete as rough
as their own tongues.
It's not the same
to get up late in the city,
find a corner shop
and buy milk that tastes of nothing much.
Back then
the taste of milk
depended on the season and the feed.
The sweetest milk

was lucerne in the spring;
while the worst I ever had
was after all the cows got through
a broken fence
and gorged themselves
on the low leaves of excluded peppertrees.
That milk was sour and bitter
as the leaves themselves,
and it was days
before the last trace disappeared.
I'd hate to think
how many years ago that happened now
but even so
the taste is still strong.
It stays there,
a detailed obsession,
like the memory of being loved.

The Bull

It was too hot for sex.
The farm was oppressed by blanket heat
and even the well-watered pot plants along the verandah
had begun to droop embarrassingly.
I looked out across the main road
and saw Col Skinner's enormous Friesian bull
alone in the small paddock.
Col's kids were there too
on the other side of the fence
lobbing bits of gravel over at the big smouldering presence.
They were too young to know what it was
that troubled the bull.
Give them a few years I thought,
they'll find out what makes him an ember.
Especially the boys.
Temperament aside however
he was the finest-looking beast this side of Tallygaroopna:
big as the tractor and black all over
except for the white patch between his eyes
that was the perfect blemish.
Looking across at him I wondered half-heartedly
What does he know of love?
with that brass ring big as a door knocker
through his nose
and the flies bothering him constantly like sex.
It wasn't so long ago I'd seen him put to the test
in a yard full of heifers
who'd been practising on each other
all the way down the lane.
As soon as the bull was let in with them he shoved his
way round the yard
sniffing at the loose wet cunts
and screwing up his nose in anticipation.
Prelims over, his prick came out dripping.
It was long, tapered and shiny red –

an exotic pickled vegetable.
When he heaved himself onto the first little jersey
she buckled alarmingly.
Col guided him in
and the old fella itself took just a few actions
to do the job,
forwards and back three times like a breadknife.
It was a sad sight really.
There must have been so many frustrated afternoons spent
in the small paddock
obsessed with the idea of this
that was happening now in the unattainable present.
If only the drenching
didn't have to be done today as well.
It started off with the bull being herded into the crush:
a tight fit
swivelling like an angry eyeball.
I couldn't see how Col would ever get the drenching gun
into that clamped mouth
but then I hadn't reckoned on Col's old man
standing there with a yard of steel pipe in his hands.
When he clobbered the bull across the face with it
there was an amazing crack
followed by a stunned silence
while the drenching got done without a hiccup.
Col's old man gave me some advice.
He said 'First thing you do with this bugger
is get his attention.'
I couldn't disagree. It had worked alright.
But still I found it hard to look at those big drops
of blood on the concrete,
and the bull staring inertly into the middle distance.
I think he knew
what he was being punished for.

Standard Hay Bales

Not the newies with their silly Van Gogh swirls
but the standard block of desiccated perfumes.
A fifty-acre paddock gridlocked with them,
each one as green and slow-bunched as a caterpillar,
the lasered space as chocked as a trailbike's tread.
Only once there's one diving on its either end
where the strong-armed baler baled dissent
(a digit raised against the uniformity on show)
while the rest is passive in its even traffic jam,
which from above becomes a repetitious Pianola roll
then in 3D is more like mid-lines of tidy droppings.
A lane is kept aside on each mowed stretch
and well before the outside windrows are pressed
the carters start to gather there like formalists.

A Farm in New York State

The fields are lying fallow now
despite the richness of their soil.
Where crops of barley used to grow
there's nothing left. It's all been spoiled.

The grain silo's an empty shell,
and trees are dying on their feet.
The only thing that's doing well
is the poison ivy underneath.

For eighteen seasons now the State
has paid this farmer just enough
to live. And things will stay like that
until the quarantine comes off.

Or if the dieldrin gets him first
his relatives receive the rest.

The Ibises

Some people say the plural is 'ibis'
but my *Dictionary for Writers and Editors*
says it's got an 'es' on the end
which is good enough for me,
and anyway that's how I always heard it said
back home at Katandra West.
Round there they were known as 'the farmer's friend'.
A good-sized flock of them
would take a ton of insects and grubs
out of the paddock in an afternoon
and at the same time aerate the soil.
No wonder they're special.
Every farmer's son learning how to shoot
is told to stay right away from the ibis.
In Egypt it's their most sacred bird.
It eats crocodile eggs for breakfast,
washes them down with only the purest water
then spends the rest of the day
probing the mud for knowledge.
And the story goes
they're so fond of living in Egypt
that if they're taken out of there
the poor things pine to death.
I couldn't be too sure about that
but I remember one time years ago
a flock of ibises hundreds strong
landing all around me in a freshly watered paddock.
The first thing I knew about it
was when the big dappled shadow rushed over me;
and then the sound,
the deepest, longest breath I'd ever heard.
As soon as each one touched down
they were straight into it,
pointedly investigating the wet pasture,
turning over interesting clues.

Real cloak-and-dagger stuff I thought.
It was a pointer to anyone there
the way that some were black
some were white
while all of them were black-and-white
and none seemed to notice.
The ibises were too busy
dipping into the language of memory
and the memory of language.
They had bodies the shape of caraway seeds
and long black bills that curved like scythes.
Suddenly they all took off.
It was probably me.
They swung round twice
as if looking for a way out
then flew directly across to Ned Wilkie's place,
leaving one last image
of a crooked smudgy line over the far trees.
I stood there thinking about it.
It wasn't much.
But it was better than a slap in the guts
with a dead fish.

The Big Goanna

Who could have guessed the big surprise
in store for Bernie Wells the day
he chased the big goanna up the tree.
If someone else had told me this
I would have said no way
a thing like that could all be true
but curiously enough for me
I was there, I saw it with my own eyes.
It happened years ago one afternoon
on Bernie's uncle's farm near Boho South
where Bernie and myself had gone
out with the twenty-twos to bring a few
rabbits home, the idea being that we
were going to make a rabbit stew
that night. But though we both
had fired at least a dozen shots
we hadn't bagged a single one.
Eventually I'd said if that's
how good we are we may as well
go home and we were just walking down a lane
not far from Bernie's uncle's house
there at the bottom of the hill
when suddenly this big goanna shot out
across the lane in front of us
and scrambled up a gum tree
on the other side. It got about
two-thirds of the way up and then
looked down at us as if to be
two-thirds of the way up that gum tree
was some sort of guarantee
of immunity from captivity. But Bernie
Wells had other things in mind and soon
he had his boots and trousers off and ran
across the lane and climbed the tree
almost as nimbly as the big goanna had.

It stayed there watching Bernie climb
until he got within about a yard
and then it crawled out on the highest limb
which would have been about thirty feet up.
It must have thought it had him beat
but good old Bernie didn't stop.
He kept on climbing right up to the top
then out along the limb towards his prey.
The big goanna watched him come
and when he wasn't far away
it simply pushed out off the branch
and plummeted towards the sticks
and leaves below and landed, crunch!,
unhurt but pretty mad, and started to flex
its tail around in a mean way the likes
of which I'd never seen before.
And instead of pissing off the bloody thing
began to climb back up the tree again!
Its tail kept making those sharp little flicks
as if it had a scorpion-like sting
while from the other end there came
a low continuous unpleasant hiss.
Poor Bernie didn't like the looks
of what he saw and he liked it even less
when the big goanna got up with him
on the branch and moved in for the bite.
There didn't seem to be any way out,
the big goanna had him stumped.
He was up about thirty feet
and too close to it for me to shoot,
but then just at the end he jumped.

The Cattle Show

The mood was tense at the annual cattle show.
Inside the pavilion a dozen well-groomed cows
were tied up along the rail while the judge
stood silently in the middle of the ring
and the owners looked on nervously. Each one had faith
that their particular cow was going to win.

To get this far each cow had had to win
their own breed's competition. They'd had to show
that they were the best of their kind. You needed faith
and a fair bit of luck just to beat the other cows
in your class. When you saw them in the ring
you realized what a close thing it was to judge.

Cruelly, if they satisfied that particular judge
and made it here for the big one their previous win
would then amount to very little if they left the ring
with only that earlier class victory to show
for their troubles. And what about all the cows
who didn't even get that far, whose owners' faith

had not been justified? Still, that's the test of faith
they say, never to stop believing. And to judge
from how the losers looked they all believed their cows
could come back here again next year and win.
There was nothing in their calm faces to show
defeat as they walked out of the ring.

Today they were gathered outside the ring
looking in at those who now had more than faith
to go on – actual runs on the board and a show
at being the 'Champion of Champions'. The judge
was taking his time to decide who would win
this great honour. He was looking at each of the cows

in turn, checking them for the things that cows
should have if they were going to be in this ring
let alone go all the way to the top and win.
The owners were standing behind with their faith
though some of them were also judging the judge
nervously and trying hard not to let it show.

Finally, when all the cows were checked the faith
of only one person in the ring was rewarded and the judge
said that to win was not the real point of the show.

Second Thoughts *on* The Georgics

You'd have to be out of your mind
to want to run a farm these days.
I mean who on earth's going to give you
a fair price for your produce?
What with the Americans flogging cheap grain
to the Russians, who can't believe their luck,
and those pricks in the EEC subsidizing
mountains and lakes of everything under
the sun. If you had the money to invest
you'd be mad to put it into farming
the way things are at the present time.
And it's not just the financial side either.
There'd hardly be a farmer in Australia
who hasn't got something wrong with his health.
Bad backs, crook knees, hernias, skin cancers,
and what about all those sprays they use,
all those herbicides and pesticides.
You can't tell me they're not bad for you.
I remember one time up at Tocumwal
staying with friends who had a rice farm.
Soon as I got there they gave me a job
standing at one end of the flooded bays
and waving an empty chaff bag
for the cropduster pilot to aim at.
He'd come in low with the sun on his wings
and go over me at powerline height.
Wading across to the next bay
a big sheet of spray would cover me
and by the time we'd finished
I was drenched to the bone with DDT.
They told me to have a good long shower
but I still felt sick as a dog later on.
          There's not so much of that sort of thing
when you grow wheat, but it's still hard work,
even if your land is over at Dookie

(the best wheat-growing soil in the state,
miles and miles of beautiful red-brown stuff).
For example, to do it properly you start
with a crop of clover and rye grass
because clover puts nitrogen into the soil.
There's a kind of satisfaction from doing things
this thoroughly, which is just as well
because there's bugger-all money in it.
The best you can hope for is to cut hay
in October and sell it to cow cockies
from Katandra, Congupna and Katamatite.
Then after the first good rain you cultivate
the ground for a crop in the autumn.
Use a neighbour's chisel plough for this –
they're too expensive to buy your own.
It's a ripper job. After hours and hours
of chewing diesel fumes you look back satisfied
at a paddock lined as neat as a fingerprint.
Wheat seed is sown in May with a drill
that also adds the phosphate as you go.
Doing this job nearly sends you broke
now that the phosphate bounty's off.
Anyway, given good rains in the spring
the crop should mature before Christmas.
Strip the grain and cart it to Dookie
where those licensed thieves the Wheat Board
have got their big row of silos.
But don't let the kids come with you.
Nev Kerr lost his youngest son down No. 5
back in the sixties. Fell in just playing
and it swallowed him like quicksand.
You burn the stubble in March.
            March is also the time for aspiring vignerons
to get their soil analysed and balanced.
That's the first expense and there's plenty
more to come, i.e. a high mesh fence
to keep out the kangaroos and rabbits,

an automatic trickle irrigation system,
tons of posts, miles of wire, the list goes on.
And not to mention all the hard work.
If you want to save a bit of money
don't buy pre-grown vines from a nursery –
you can easily pick up the cuttings
when someone else is pruning theirs.
Stick them in a bed for a year
and most of them will strike and send out roots.
That helps, but there's still a lot more trouble
and expense. Once the vines are bearing
you have to cover each one with a fine mesh
to keep off those bloody silvereyes,
and you have to spray for mildew
and keep an eye out for other vine diseases.
Then there's the things you can't control:
a good shower of hail strips everything,
severe frost burns the leaves, so does bushfire.
And even if you get through all this
and make the wine, there's still no guarantee
you're going to come out ahead financially.
Thank Christ for tax write-offs.
            Each evening after the news
it's important to watch the weather.
The best forecasts are the ABC and GMV6.
The ABC gives you the broad picture
while GMV6 has the detailed local stuff.
Don't worry about the Melbourne commercials –
those sexy weathergirls never give you
half the information you can get
from safe avuncular types on the ABC.
But it's also worth remembering that the ads
on commercial stations are good weather-signs,
i.e. the appearance of the first flyspray ad
tells you that summer is on the way
and seeing Vulcan oil-heater ads again
warns you to get ready for colder weather.

That's generally the time, during May,
when the cows round Katandra are drying off.
Drench them for fluke and give them a spell
for a couple of months. If you're lucky
you can get them agistment at Caniambo
or somewhere like that. It's better for the cows
and it gives the home paddocks a rest.
But if you can't get them somewhere else
don't be stingy with their hay.
There's nothing worse than half-starved stock.
I wouldn't hesitate to call the RSPCA
if I saw a neighbour was holding back.
Half a bale per day is what they need –
and make sure it's good tucker, not cheap stuff.
And when you're feeding out be careful
not to leave loose baling-twine in the paddock.
Cows can choke to death on it,
especially now that it's made of plastic.
This is the off-season, when you tune fences
and reopen drains that have started to heal.
Good while it lasts but all too soon
the cows are dropping calves around the clock
and you're back in the milking shed
with the milk-mad cats under your feet
and some little bitch of a jersey
has kicked her cups off into the shit
just when you've got your hands full
with some other slut who's done the same,
and the tanker driver's leaning on the rail
explaining about his son at university,
'I tell you what, these fucking intellectuals,
they couldn't track an elephant through the snow.'
Then after you've finished in the shed
it's time to go and feed the poddies.
They all come jostling up to you
as if you've just kicked the winning goal,
but any money there'll be one of them

won't drink. You'll have to get her head down
in the bucket and push your milky fingers
into her mouth before she'll start sucking.
Years later, in a rented room in the city,
you might remember that insistent tugging
and feel yourself drawn back there
to those wet paddocks imbued with light,
but right now there's work to be done
because October is the busiest month.
The cows are up to peak production,
the irrigation starts again, and you also
have to cut, rake and press the hay.
If the cut hay is dry you should rake
and press it at night. The dew means you don't
lose as much leaf off the clover and grass.
Certainly never rake hay on a windy day.
As soon as you lift the rows they blow
all over the paddock. For carting in
wear chaps, watch out for thistles in the bales
(even snakes), don't smoke up on the load
and don't do your back lifting the wrong way.
When you're having trouble at the hayshed
get a stack plan out of the *Weekly Times*.
If you're cluey you can make one up yourself.
The basic idea is to bind the stack.
Remember once you've finished building it
to keep a check for spontaneous combustion.
Shove your arm in. If there's too much heat
pull the whole thing apart straight away.
Better that than the local fire brigade.
Another thing to watch out for in October
is the clover growth that causes bloat.
It's always a blow to lose a cow that way –
squeezed to death from the inside,
hugely round with legs jutting everywhere
like some washed-up unexploded mine.
If you get there in time you can try

104

stabbing her flank with a bloat valve
though it's not something I'd really recommend.
Too many times it kills the cow anyway.
I once saw a vet at Waaia put a match
to the gas that came whooshing out.
The effect was a long blue tongue of flame
and the cow died mostly from fright.
They say he did it again at Marungi
and someone dobbed him in and he got struck off.
So the best thing is to get in early
and spray your pasture with bloat oil.
You can also pour it into the drinking troughs
and paint the cows' flanks with it.
In December you follow up by slashing
to take off seed-heads left over from grazing
and this encourages new shoots, which you then
strip-graze with an electric fence.
Slashing's an easy job but for God's sake
be careful of the PTO. Harry Thompson
lost an index finger just pulling out a bit
of hay-band while the thing was still engaged.
Old Harry was pretty relaxed about it though.
He turned off the tractor, tied up the dogs,
and only then drove himself into town.
              Of course, you don't need machinery
to get hurt. Think of breaking a horse.
Imagine how easy it is to get kicked
shoeing a fizzy mare for the first time
or even just walking round behind her
if you don't stick close and let her know
where you are. Keep your hand on her
as you go, work reassuringly from the side,
and don't make any sudden movements.
You see, apart from anything else,
it's better to get kicked from in close
than it is to cop one back at full swing.
The best thing is to handle the horse

constantly while you're breaking her in.
Rub her and scratch her all over,
lift the feet, cover the eyes, the ears –
get her used to your presence and smell.
Only then do you start breaking to saddle.
Firstly, just lean across her back for a while.
When she's used to that, throw on a rug
and go inside for a cup of tea.
You probably won't find the next step
in any textbook, but it's a good one.
Put a dog or a cat on the horse's back
and try to make it stay up there.
Horses have a natural fear of animals
attacking them like this in the wild
so it's a good discipline for them to learn.
Next, you start getting on and off yourself,
both sides. And you can even slide off
back down the rump – but slowly of course
so she always knows where you are.
Now put the saddle on for the first time,
securely, with a crupper, and leave it on
(though maybe put it on and take it off
a few times before you tighten the girth).
When she seems to have accepted the saddle
upset her so she bucks and has a go at it;
then calm her down and reassure her.
You should be right now to get up into
the saddle and start moving around the yard
using both the reins and leg signals.
(Someone leading on another horse is good here.)
Teach her to come to either hand,
to walk and stop, to trot, and to canter
slowly both ways round the lunging-yard.
After that you're ready for some fun, so get out
into the paddock and have a good gallop.
(This isn't exactly Xenophon but it'll do.)
You can be in the saddle within a day

but the full education takes years.

      Same with dogs. It's frustrating really
the way they reach their peak
just when they're disappearing over the hill.
That's why it's important always to have
a young dog coming on. Make sure
they're well-bred – a champion doesn't cost
any more to feed than some old mongrel
and it's the same for the vet or anything.
The best place you can start is to get the pup
at eight weeks and break the dog/dog thing.
Tie him up overnight behind a far shed
and don't worry about how much he howls.
When you go down there in the morning
he's pleased to see you and you begin
to form the bond between man and dog.
So then you go on to the basic disciplines;
the language of spoken commands –
Fetch 'em up! Go away back! Get out of it!
Stop! Stop dead! OK Speak up! Push 'em up! –
and that other language, the bird-like one.
(A few years ago I was in a European capital
staying in this big barn of a youth hostel.
The dining room was packed. You could hear
dozens of different languages being spoken.
I finished up at a table in a corner
talking to this New Zealand bloke
who was also off the land. Somehow we began
comparing whistle-signals, just to see
what the similarities and the differences were.
We exchanged the short sharp ones,
the low mournful ones, the two-parters,
the shrill excited repeaters, the curvers,
the tremblers, the piercers, and so on.
All around us conversations stopped.
The polyglots stared and listened in dismay.
What was this language of almost-echoes?)

Anyway, after they've got the basic stuff
it's just years and years of fine tuning,
like the horses, like nearly everything.
Give them meat and water in the evening
and wash your hands after you've handled them –
you can catch terrible things from dogs.
There's one strain of hydatid tapeworm
that gets into your system and works right up
into your brain and then starts eating it!

      But when you talk about hygiene
it's pigs you have to be most careful with.
They're more susceptible to sickness
and disease than any other farm animal
(though they're actually one of the cleanest).
Make sure their pens have a concrete floor
with good gutters and a decent fall
so they can be washed out easily,
and try to have weld-mesh separating them
rather than timber, which can hold disease
(and because, given half a chance, most pigs
will chew their way out of a timber pen).
No names, but back home one of our neighbours
was into pigs in a pretty big way
and the bugger did none of these things.
So it wasn't surprising when all his sows
came down with a dose of leptospirosis.
There was what they call an 'abortion storm'.
All the piglets were born prematurely
and being weak they died soon afterwards.
He treated the whole herd with streptomycin
but obviously it was too late by then.
He even tried burning the infected carcasses
round the back of his machinery shed
but that was just another balls-up.
They didn't burn very well and dogs
carried pieces of them all over the district.
You'd find some half-burnt bit of pig

down a back paddock miles away,
or worse, you'd find your three-year-old kid
playing with one on the front doorstep.
And of course what happened in the end
was that other herds contracted the disease
and people started getting sick with it too.
Some farmers were laid up for weeks.
All in all it was a real disaster.
          So you see, it's not just boutique beer
out on the verandah after the wool cheque.
There's any number of things can go wrong
no matter what type of farming you do,
and the only thing you can be sure of
is that you'll never get a fair return
for all the hard hours you put in.
They might be useful for writing down
a bit of didactic pastoral stuff
in the language that reminds you of home
but that's about where it ends.
If Virgil was here I reckon he'd agree.
Even keeping bees is a waste of time –
better to take your honey where you find it.

In an American Wood

We've all been dispossessed.
It happens for the first time
under lights at the institute of separations.
There's no rational reason to be alarmed
but we cry and cry anyway.
Later, when the cycle of relinquishment is well established
we keep a sullen silence
walking through an unfamiliar type of National Park.
Human interference abounds.
There are big signs at every turn
proclaiming the dangers of Grizzly bears.
(Apparently they're quick and humourless
and they'll kill for honey.)
And strewn along the levee bank
are bits of cars, soft-drink cans and aerosols.
It's a disconcerting vision,
like Manhattan stripped of everything except the plumbing.
Through slender calibrated trunks
I can see what seems to be a big tangle of blackberries,
a rising equally up and out
so smug in its fluent evasiveness.
Is 'last gasp' tautological?
Yesterday I saw a loony drop his pants
and defecate in the foyer of the Waldorf Hysteria
or whatever its name is.
We've all been taken away from something.
'De-centered' I think the Americans call it,
and they even have a documentary to prove it.
Every time you turn over a bush
there's another camera crew wanting to make
something that's never been made before.
This one's trying to photograph memory.
Last year they found a dinosaur round here
perfectly fossilized in coal,
remains of swamp grass still mashed up in its mouth

and nothing to suggest
what made it die just standing there flat-footedly.
The giant bones were all intact,
suspended by the former oakwood forest
and mighty brittle with the passing of so many years.
Apparently if you get squirted by a skunk
the only way to take the smell off
is by soaking in a bathful of tomato juice.
Whatever thing it is we miss
the commentators say it's gone, we can't go back.
According to the tourist information map
this little clearing here
is where a village stood three hundred years ago.

Superphosphate

With more cogs and chains and trapdoors
than a mediaeval torture chamber
the super-spreader nudges cautiously
underneath the twenty-five-ton super-bin
raised up on sci-fi giant insect legs
that from a distance make the bin
seem like an oil-rig out of water.
Up close however it's only like itself,
a hull of welded plates creating space
to hold a powerful tonic for the paddocks.
The spreader gets aligned first time,
then not without a burst of language
the blunted bottom doors scissor apart
and one bone-coloured ton cascades
into the rictus caked with settled dust
from loads of other fertilizer stints.
Arcs of suspension flatten out
and under strain the Fergie leads
along the track and into a paddock
primed for cost-effective distribution.
No post-election cut in subsidies
can stop the recommended process now
and with a kick the gyros are engaged.
It begins in a whirl of grating noise
like something desperate scouring metal
and soon is taken over by a cloud
of dry weight that burns the eyes.
Below the cloud off-white small pebbles
are flung viciously against the grass blades
and form a layer just visible enough
to be the nearest thing to light snow
that most Australian paddocks ever see.
Despite the finer super's airborne acid
the cattledogs can't keep themselves away.
Their noses run, their eyes fill up

and when they test the creamy pellets
with a reckless tongue the only thing
that's worse is an electric fence.
But still they follow close behind,
a couple a small-town gadabouts
who can't resist whatever's happening
even if it makes them sneeze like mad.
Each paddock gets a share of this
until the bin gives up the ghostly stuff
and disappears then like a spacecraft
leaving scanty cryptic evidence behind,
a set of perfect footprints in the yard
where each square foot of half-inch steel
came down hard to break the gravel up
like making super out of phosphate rock.

Five Thousand Acre Paddock

There was only one
tree in all that space and he
drove straight into it.

The Map

The map is just about as old as memory.
It has more options than a young man leaving home,
more lines and broken veins than an old man's face.

Exactly in the centre are the clustered names
that vowels and consonants were first tried out on
before the dumb cartographies could be defined.

And though the map seems two-dimensional
that centre is depressed enough for simple things
to keep slipping back into its lowest common point.

Spread out amongst the late-afternoon shadows
the map is covering everything that matters.
The way things are it can't be folded up again.

The Dry

Last Christmas up at Yabba North
the silos went without their grain
and farmers watched an empty sky
as if there still might be some rain.

The faded flags of paddocks lay
symmetrically around the town
with all their wheat and barley crops
like matches scattered on the ground.

Dry dams became engraved as hard
as big inverted turtle-shells;
and hungry sheep were packed into
the truckie's mobile prison shelves.

Some days a willy-willy made
of topsoil from the past would lean
then stagger sadly back across
a place it had already been.

Whenever loads of cattle-feed
came down the Dookie-Yabba line
the cockatoos would gather there
to see what spillage they could find.

And if a sheep or cow pegged out
its carcass darkened then with flies
and those much darker shapes of crows
who always started with the eyes.

Shotgun Distinction

It has a double-barrelled lead-brained way
of getting to the heart of things,

a big-eyed literal-minded knack
for seeing them in their true duality

especially when cocked with cockiness.
The straight end looks out cold as metal,

its eyes too close together to inspire trust
and the irises dark with loathing.

One thoughtless rush of blood
and those eyes can fill with fire,

a loud unnatural extension of the eyes
behind the wooden sculpted other end,

the butt that butts the shooter's shoulder
like an angry billygoat with two long horns.

If the receiving end bleeds thoughtlessly
it means the spiral of dichotomies

has got some life left in it yet.
For instance, were they ducks returning

to their reeds just as the evening light drew in
or were they rabbits feeding cautiously

not far outside their safety bushes
while the morning sun aimed barrels of light?

Even those darker barrels are only
a well-matched pair of unidentical twins.

See how the right is half-choked
for more spread and less quick-shadowed distance

while the left has a narrower vision
to go after whatever got away.

And see each time how they present
the hardest choice of perfect clones of lead,

perhaps a number-eight to let off first
and then a number-three to follow up.

If both are fired at once
the result is two lines of unequal length.

The not-so-random patterns they make
approximate in miniature the spread of ducks

returning to their reeds at sunset
or the spread of rabbits feeding on grass

decorated with pellets of morning dew.
Only some of the shot will hit

some of the spread of ducks or rabbits,
and what goes on travelling

will be the same on both disrupted sides –
a careful pattern with a hole in it.

The only difference will be
the time they take to reach the earth.

Gestalt Test

What better Gestalt test
than a herd of Friesian cows?
Their black-and-white abstractions
are just made for interpretation.
Every time you look there's some
new order emerging from the chaos,
while things you thought you saw
are back behind stark camouflage.
It's a jumbled jigsaw puzzle,
a game of continental shift
in which the shifts are instantaneous.
Here's one where South America
is being pushed over the top
by a huge upside-down Tasmania
not long before she gets eclipsed
by a well-rounded map of India –
a soft udder with one large teat.
Suddenly there's a snow storm
across a big-nosed Dalmatian's face,
and when the worst is over
the ice floes start breaking up.
In summer it's more likely to be
big wet leaves stuck on flanks,
or more subtle smaller foliage
about to be blown into patterns
by the particle-filled jet streams
swirling round the rear cleavage.
Others are more New York School
and you might be tempted to say
'A five-year-old could do better',
though this one is indisputably good
with its sombre painterly shapes
as monumental as Motherwell's
'Elegy to the Spanish Republic'.
The lesser school is straight landscape,

usually something pretty simple –
a few suggestions of foreground
and, inked in heavily behind,
a great jagged mountain range.
Then there's always one cow
who has a rather exotic print,
say, something austere and Japanese –
looking over one smooth boulder
at a still lake just on sunset.
Sometimes these metamorphoses
happen so quickly and so slickly
you can't believe your eyes.
And if the Friesians could speak
they'd probably say 'We told you so'.
For though they see in monochrome
they know it's a mixed-up world
where all is not black-and-white.

The Discs

To go back purposefully to the big machinery shed
and start the tractor up,
and then reverse the tractor over to the discs
enmeshed in long grass there beside the diesel tank,
and hitch them to hydraulic sway-bars
taking care to snap the safety pins in place.

To travel slowly down the bottom lane
and feel the steering light and ineffectual
because of all that weight held up behind,
and to hear loose steel crash awkwardly
through each dry pothole, dip
or stretch of corrugation smudged with gravel dust.

To come to a chained five-bar gate and stop
and swing down off the tractor in one sharp movement
landing with a crunch on Rossi workboots,
and then to swing the gate wide open
and stand there for a moment
looking thoughtfully at thirty acres of rested soil.

To drive into the paddock then
and drop the discs down heavily into the dirt,
fix the self-adjusting height control
and set off in the lowest ratio
with the throttle pulled back halfway,
the engine and the discs complaining noisily.

To stay there through the day
working clockwise inwards from the fence
with only noise fatigue for company,
the chocolate dust becoming mud in sweaty hair,
the steady sun sunburning tops of ears, backs of hands
and heating up the brain inside the hatless head.

To get off now and then
and take a lengthy swig from the dripping canvas waterbag

that hangs from bar-weights at the front,
then drive across to where the forty-four of diesel stands
and pump more pungent diesel in
using the squeaky hand-pump screwed into the top.

To finish just on dark
with teal ducks going overhead toward the swamp
and gently angled lines of dense sunlight
investigating rows of upturned soil
that all lead ineluctably
back into the centre of the rich paddock.

Pastoral Feature Film

It doesn't matter what the critics say.
As long as market forces still exist
the country boys are guaranteed to pay.

For most of them the urban time since they
were taken from their farm has been a waste.
It doesn't matter what the critics say.

Let's make the film revolve around the day
the farm was sold. Who needs a publicist?
The country boys are guaranteed to pay.

We'll load them up with every last cliché
and give the storyline a facile twist.
It doesn't matter what the critics say

about our cynical approach, the way
we're cleaning up on someone else's past.
The country boys are guaranteed to pay

because it's all they've got. They've been away
from home too long and now they can't resist.
It doesn't matter what the critics say.
The country boys are guaranteed to pay.

From *Up On All Fours*

The End of the Season

The sadness of the cows
is all too evident.
Their heads are down,
tears deepen their eyes,
and when the farmer
finally herds his herd
into the milking shed
he only gets a small
nostalgic bucketful –
the last one for the year.
Too much imbued with loss
to be used for butter
the warm yellow milk
is taken behind the shed
and given to the pigs.

The Scarifier

There's no one way that best describes
the scarifier after it
rolls back from tearing up the grass.
A rigid grid of broken ribs,
two wings designed to fly through dirt,
and rows of nipples fouled with grease,

it's a dangerous moving stage
where anyone who slipped would find
themselves impaled on crescent steel
that narrows to the sharpened edge
of half a clay-encrusted tine.
But when it's clean and standing still

the scarifier looks more like
an instrument for swaying those
who have some trouble with their faith,
a mediaeval torture rack,
a bed of knives and pointy toes
for making people see the truth.

It lurks like that behind the shed
until the next year's autumn rain
comes down as straight and crowded as
the stalks of wheat it helped to seed
and then it takes the field again
with forty sets of faithful claws.

A Note from Mindi Station

The isolation seemed so reasonable:
three days of stasis on a broken track
with big cogs grinding in low ratio,
a survey map to make it possible,
strong ancient land-speak on the radio
and unexpected camels staring back.

Since then the North Cottage has been a base,
a kind of focus in this blur of scrub.
It's near a dried-up section of the creek
about five miles from where the homestead is.
Their daughter brings supplies out once a week
and talks about some things she can't describe:

the strangely ferrous colours of the soil,
the transitory displays that follow rain,
and more than any other thing, the sky –
its depth, its range, its overwhelming scale.
It has a presence she can't explain –
not what it is, but what it might imply.

She says she loves to watch the tiny jets
adhering to their flight-path eight miles up
and wonder where they might be headed for.
By straining you can just make out their shape
but nothing of the isolated roar.
They're silent as a particle of dust.

Today a sparrow hawk was hovering there.
Its legs had been let down with claws outstretched,
the wings had worked themselves into a blur,
the head was changing settings like a switch;
but what was fixed in place was one small bird,
which might have been the pivot of the world.

After the Shearing

By mid-afternoon the corrugated shed, cathedral-big,
is empty except for the smell of lanolin and piss,
the same sweet mixture that every year now
for over a hundred years has seasoned the timber
at sheep height – the gates and posts and pen rails
and the bottoms of the giant Murray Pine poles
all of them treated with this by-product of work.
Applied and rubbed in unwillingly in the crowded week
it makes the sawn lengths almost human to handle.
The light is something like it too – worn and dull.
Outside in the glare a semitrailer loaded with
the monumental bales of wool is heading off to town
and thousands of sheep are leaving the night paddock
humiliated, only half the size they were a week ago
and taking with them their bright medical colours –
the new whites, the new reds. We drive behind them
in the ute while the farmer's son-in-law tells us
what he thinks about these staggering animals.
'They're all man-made. Nothing like they used to be.
You couldn't let them go now. They'd get fly strike
or sick. Dogs maybe. The wool'd grow over their eyes!'
The paddock extends for miles in front of us
to a faint hard edge where it stops the sky.
We notice a kestrel above the mob, held there
by hunger, waiting for something to be disturbed,
for movement to show what was hidden in stillness.
And almost immediately the sheep do their job.
Swinging down in a fast arc the kestrel clips the ground,
performs a long involuntary hop unbalancing herself,
comes good by holding out scary slowdown wings
then flaps off in a trance to the nearest fence post
with her trapeze-partner mouse caged in one claw.
At first she bends forward and picks at it rapidly
like a sewing machine but then loses interest,
tilts back, and watches us pass quite close.

She reappears in the sky about half a mile later
just as the sheep throw up a pair of stubble quails
who flutter around in tandem for a moment calling
'pippy-wheep! pippy-wheep!' and then dive under
our low rolling ute, the only available shelter
in this nibbled-down paddock as big as a home county.
We worry about wheels and the dangerous exhaust
but the quails seem at home there, flitting out
for a glance and coming back with elastic speed.
They make the same eventful noises under us
that swallows make when nesting in a roof –
muffled scratches and rubs, the odd knock and cry –
and while we go on like this it's tempting to imagine
their adoption lasting longer than the paddock's length
were it not for that kestrel shadowing our progress.

Milk Cream Butter

He'd get up every morning before the sun
had cleared the treeline on his neighbour's creek,
and while the sound of magpies trickled in
the slightly opened window of his room
he'd take whatever clothes he'd worn all week,
a tattered pile that mostly smelled of him,
and shake them out and put them on again.
That time of day the paddock by the house
was brittle with a covering of frost
so when he went to get his seven cows
it left a zig-zag trail of darker prints
where the silver grass got crushed beneath his boots.
The cows would wander down along a fence
that led them through a set of open gates
and when they'd turn into the narrow lane
he'd notice how their cautious feet would mince
the gravel-filling with the mud again.
Arriving at the milking shed the queue
of weighted cows would always be the same.
They'd practised twice a day and now they knew
the sequence and the distance off by heart.
They knew the routine of the single bail
and after that how far to keep apart.
So there was nothing much he had to do
except to chain them in and wet the teats
then draw the lines of milk into the pail
between his legs, a tight metallic gasp
that changed into exquisite frothy breaths.
In less than half an hour he'd have them done
and while they sauntered back the way they'd come
he'd go out to the separating room
and tip the previous morning's creamless milk
into two pig troughs that used to be a drum
and then he'd pour each bucketful of warm
fresh milk into a metal cooling dish.

Beside them was a wooden butter-churn
that looked like some sideshow magician's prop.
He'd fill it up with sour cream and turn
the handle steadily until the fat
began to float in globules on the top.
A final rapid stirring firmed them up
he'd slide a bucket underneath, then pull
the plug and let the buttermilk escape
before he'd fill the small vat nearly full
of water, rinse the butter clean, then add
some salt and take the soapy mixture out
in handfuls, which he'd torture like a rag,
removing with a twist the final drops.
The rest was just a kind of copyright.
He'd press the butter into one-pound pats
with an emu imprinted on the tops
denoting him, and when the job was done
he'd notice that those blocks of golden light
were glowing deeper than the early sun.

The Tail Paddock

After six weeks of milky growth and joy
the lambs have their tails ringed
by a little rubber muscle
that cuts the feeling off in a few hours
and the tail in about ten days.
Such a loss is more than just a tail.
It's also innocence.
The stumpy lambs go from playful carelessness
to a state of numb resentment
where all they can do
is hang around their mother's smell
and look at the world their paddock
now decorated with hundreds of woolly tails
going slightly green in the spring sunshine
that shimmers on the wings of crows
who've gathered there to sort through the tails
and finding one fly off
with it dangling innocently
almost the way it used to.

The Rock Paddocks

The fences that define the paddocks here
are made of basalt rocks that used to spread
across the spaces they now enclose.
A hundred years ago someone had to clear
these rocks with nothing but a horse-drawn sled
and stack them into uncemented rows

that gave the random country Shape and Form.
Since then the earth has strangely given up
another covering of rocks the same
as what was cleared, a generation born
so cautiously they never interrupt
the Aspect that their forebears helped to tame.

They happen over centuries and stop
when all they have to push against is air.
So slow the paddocks are taken by surprise.
And though it's time to strip this useless crop
the man who owns the paddocks doesn't care.
He knows there's more already on the rise.

Rural Affairs

The family farm is up for sale:
the wheat can't grow as fast as debt.
Overseas, our markets fail
while politicians lend regret.

The wheat can't grow as fast as debt.
It fades from green to bristling gold
while politicians lend regret
that wheat like this remains unsold.

It fades from green to bristling gold
in just a fraction of the time
that wheat like this remains unsold.
The current import figures climb

in just a fraction of the time
it takes a dog to sniff the wind.
The current import figures climb
until the market's disciplined.

It takes a dog to sniff the wind.
No-one else has got the skill.
Until the market's disciplined
the Treasurer should close the till.

No-one else has got the skill.
The commentators all agree
the Treasurer should close the till
and tell us where he hides the key.

The commentators all agree
they have a special role to come
and tell us where he hides the key.
The truth is always troublesome.

They have a special role to come.
It's going to mean explaining how
the truth is always troublesome:
a pen is better than a plough.

It's going to mean explaining how
these circumstances came about.
A pen is better than a plough
if some growers are driven out.

These circumstances came about
because the magic market said
if some growers are driven out
the pool of benefits will spread.

Because the magic market said
'We need a level playing field!'
the pool of benefits will spread
across the land like truth revealed.

'We need a level playing field!'
Overseas, our markets fail.
Across the land, like truth revealed,
the family farm is up for sale.

A Half-remembered Visit

There was an early mudbrick homestead out the back
sentinelled by a couple of sinewy redgums, their bark
coming away just like the render on the chimney.
The foot-thick walls were cracking at dramatic angles
before they went back into the familiar earth,
and weeds had grabbed a chance in silted-up gutters.
All that needed to happen was for the roof to go
and then the chronic phase would move into acute.
For the moment though the family used it as a place
to store things they couldn't quite throw out.
One room was a puzzle of broken harnesses, bridles,
saddles, cruppers and girth straps, stiff and heavy
with the smell of themselves and long-gone horses.
In another room an open tea-chest on its side
was dealing out old photographs of groups of people
in brown Victorian light. You could tell by looking
that all these people had been dead for years.
Outside in the yard, their descendant the farmer
showed his visitors a family of stables, barns and sheds.
Abandoned implements lay like skeletons in the grass.
Nothing, it seemed, had been used for a long time
except the sayings and stories that came to mind
each time he walked out there into his identity.
He stood beside what used to be a chook shed
and pointed to a rafter where bone and leather
remnants still crouched, unmoved since the day
his wife, running the farm on her own while he
was at the war, had shot an egg-obsessed goanna.
This is what the shed had come to mean to him,
and it was like this no matter where you looked:
each place and object around the overgrown yard
was a way in for him to some particular memory.
The whole farm had become a museum of the mind.
It didn't matter to him that it was so run-down.
'There's nothing as permanent as a temporary job,'

he said, quite happily, and pointed out a few examples:
gates rough-hinged with wire, sheets of roofing iron
held down by big stones, and over at the dam
a piece of stocking as the filter on the pump.
Between the yard and dam stood three peach trees,
each one framed in its own mesh-wire cage
that was there to keep out the birds and possums.
All the isolation and symmetry they'd been given
made those trees look somehow more significant
than anything else we'd seen that afternoon.
It should have been easy enough to walk away from
but it was kind of puzzling, even then. There was
a feeling that something had already been forgotten.

J.H.W. Mules

They're mulesing up at Wilga Downs
with hairy fists and special knives.
The ewes are making urgent sounds
before they're partly skinned alive

and underneath the frightened shed
the mix of dirt and pellet dung
is getting damp with drops of blood:
the product of a job well done.

Out in the yard some sickly ewes
have gone to ground and died of shock
though farmers never mind a few
like this to tighten up the flock.

The thousands more that aren't too weak
to have their breeches opened wide
against the profit-wound of strike
let farmers take it in their stride.

No doubt it was the same for Mules,
detached and pensive at his desk.
Ideas we have for animals
are only monstrous in the flesh.

The Hoop Snake

Out in that country north of the range,
that marginal grazing land where one
head of cattle per ten square miles
is the rule of thumb in a good year,
that hoof-and-mouth-degraded open country,
lives the hoop snake, terror of the plains.

Forty years ago my father started work
on a station of the plains (his first job
in a country stocked with Irish names
but not much else that seemed like home),
a station where the lazy jackeroos
were quick to give the new boy some advice.

Watch out for snakes! They rear up and bite
their tail and make themselves into a hoop
that comes rolling faster than you can run!
He watched out all right. Everywhere he went.
Round the stockyards, in at the homestead,
down by the creek and out in the paddocks

he watched. He'd never seen a snake before
but when the moment came it was quick
as a snake: something that didn't have to be
learned. It went back deeper than that.
He was fixing up a boundary fence (the wire
was pulled through as taut as it could go –

one more arm wrestle with the strainer
and the wire would have lashed out and struck)
when he noticed that a small dark shiny pool
had been poured onto a patch of open ground
not far from where the next dropper went.
Straight away he saw it for what it was,

as if he'd dealt with snakes all his life.
A recognition that was waiting to be felt.

He worked his way around it, stepping lightly,
slowly getting closer, slowly getting braver,
never sliding his attention from the centre
of the sleeping spiral when out of time

St Patrick help me now in all this dry
it flowed awake with many faithful muscles
straightening out across his homesick boots!
He reacted back too late, an older man,
and lashed his length of eight-gauge fencing wire
across the middle of the six-foot snake.

Broken but still with three dangerous feet
it took another whipping then a boot heel
before my father saw it for what it was:
a line of common memory lying in the dust.
Bent unnaturally now like the length of wire
it never got a chance to make the hoop.

European Carp

The way that rabbits bred across the land,
a frantic follow-on to Austin's twelve,
so too these toothless low-life types have spawned
right through the Murray-Darling waterways.
Escaping from a pond in New South Wales
they paralleled the post-war immigrant
in timing, drive and so-called lack of taste
by filling spots the locals didn't want
and making do with anything at first.
Ironically these other Euro-spills,
or waves, turned out to be the only ones
who'd eat a fish like this: all clumsy scales
and muddy flesh impossible with bones.
Apparently they'd poach it up in stock
and some of them were even said to think
it was a kind of aphrodisiac.
Nowadays their children's middle-class cuisine
excludes such items from the peasant past
while carp have grown in number, size and range,
displaced at least a dozen other fish,
and been officially declared a pest.
At times they've been so thick that kids have shot
them in the water with their twenty-twos
and in the Murray swimmers standing still
have felt a barbelled vacuum on their toes.
In Yanko Creek they suckle at the edge.
Lined up like rows of piglets on a sow
they filter all the goodness from the sludge
and cloud the water so that plants don't grow.
Of course there's no surprise in any of this.
As soon as those experimental few
were flooded into main connecting streams
the system's damage was as good as done.
There was no way that it could stay the same.
But how on earth did European carp
get into Charlie Hughes' remotest dam?

The Rabbit Trap

So tense and yet it doesn't mind waiting,
sometimes for years: a quiet disused track
becoming in an instant the theatre
of sharp loud pain, of ready rusty teeth
embedded in the foot of some bushwalker
who never hurt another living thing.

So crude and yet it tricks the nimblest creatures,
jumping shut before instinct or reflexes
can swerve the victim from its struggling death,
and making no distinction between the one
intended animal and all the others;
the different species caught in this debate.

So fast and yet it takes the longest time
of any butcher's steel to do its job –
the sufferer might hang on for days
not knowing if the counting heart will stop
or if the smell of human predator
will come to bring the process up to date.

So sensitive and yet it is unfeeling,
always reacting badly to the slightest
pressure on the blood-stained centre plate,
the stage where little tragedies are played out
while back in some warm spot the mother's young
stare out as the world closes in on them.

After a Dry Stretch

The rain appears, as always, from the west.
Behind the mountain ranges it seems at first
to be a bigger, purpler, more distant range:
a counterpoint for some corellas, their wings
turning whitenesses on and off, unsynchronized.
Soon, almost quietly going about its business,
a marriage of elements descends the foothill slopes
and settles in for the day on the flat country.
In minutes your field of view is brought up close:
through rain there is only more rain further back
and cow shapes with their colours all washed out.
Reconstituting paddocks, eliminating dust
the rain is what was promised by machines.
Remembering its way by feel down gullies
it gathers colour, plaited milky brown, and reaches
the creek all stirred up, back together at last.
Getting through barricades of its own making,
hastily putting up new ones out of any loose wood,
water-rat-matted coats of dead rushes, bright plastics,
it repeats itself, stuttering in the tight situations
and growing in confidence over the broad deep lengths,
determined not to be drawn out in the next transition.
Now in the paddocks there are frogs, unpuffed,
still sluggish and flecked with dirt. Their credo
is sequential, 'Add water, reproduce, avoid snakes'.
Even the big ones are learning all over again:
they react by mating with the toe of your boot
when you give them a nudge. Their talkback
is regular as the rain, though lower and sharper.
Not far away, in a galvanized machinery shed
diesel is cascading into the tractor already hitched
to a ton and a half of crop seed on wheels.
From inside the amplifying shed it sounds like
hard seed is raining down on the corrugated roof.
A nail hole lets in star-small light, and raindrops.

More bags of seed are ready on a loading platform:
they might be sandbags stacked before a flood.
The farmer looks out at his unwritten paddocks,
relieved that all the weather-chat is finished
and that soon he'll be out there for days on end
filling the fallow space with standard lines.
The yard dog chases the old tab across bags
of seed. They both know it's only a game.
Over at the house too, the rain is happiness
for water is chortling into the big tank,
smoke is unravelling from the year's first fire
and mushrooms are forming in the minds of children.

Driving Through the Mallee

The long loose lines of fence wire climbed then slipped
hypnotically from post to post both sides.
Above them in the paddocks to the left
new power lines did the same with slower strides.

Occasionally a tree would interrupt
the rhythm of these lines, providing some
almost unwanted interest while we tried
to guess the type – most times a sugar gum.

And once there was a lazy broken line
diagonally across a paddockful
of stalks, and this turned out to be some sheep
packed into rolls of muscly-looking wool.

There wasn't much else, just stillness and space.
And in the car the only movement was
the empty stubbies rolling on the floor,
like wind chimes tinkling in a quiet breeze.

The charcoal highway and the tinder crops
it set a firebreak between were so
unvaried that you often felt you'd been
along that stretch of road a while ago.

Round three we stopped for petrol in a town
the same as all those towns – a wide main street
of fibro houses, dusty shops and pubs
surrounded by uninterrupted wheat.

Not much was happening at that time of day.
Across the road in someone's vacant lot
a chestnut horse was rolling in the dust,
contortedly, as though it had been shot

and through a window of the nearest pub
more horses ran through television light

in front of tables crowned with upturned chairs.
The only individual in sight,

the service station man who filled the tank,
was sullen to the point of being rude.
He snatched the pair of twenty-dollar notes
and handed back the change without a word.

A few more miles from there we stopped again,
this time to watch a hawk suspended near
the road, its beak and ready claws all hooked
and shiny dark, its wings held out to steer

nowhere against the breeze. It stayed like that
for several minutes in a single spot,
so still a rifle could have picked it off.
And then it dropped as though it had been shot

and disappeared into the waist-high crop.
There was an unfamiliar squeak, a pause,
the sifting sound you often hear in wheat
and then the hawk flew up with empty claws.

Erosion and Salinity

What used to be a paddock
is now a kind of chart.
A deep erosion-split
runs through the middle
crooked as if the page
were being torn apart,

erratically up and down
as if that jagged line
were some financial graph
tracing the water table's
salt-productive rise
and the farmer's dry decline.

His problems all stem back
to the indifferent ease
with which the bulldozer
levelled off his topsoil
and cleared the paddock
of its water-funnel trees.

Though that started things
it's really no-one's fault.
There wasn't much around
to show how things change.
What used to be a frost
is now a covering of salt.

Three Pig Diseases

1. Baby Pig Disease

The scene is like Nativity.
A sweet clear night outside
while in the shed the farmer shines a torch
so that the vet, down on his hands and knees,
can move each shivering handful
closer to the row of teats.
The mother, groaning on her bed of hay,
seems beached beyond their knowledge or experience.
Pressed up against the wall
she stares into a painful distance.
There's nothing that the farmer or the vet can do.
Life is offering itself from those teats,
swelling, dripping, souring
and the piglets just won't drink.
It's like an obstinate belief.
Over the next few days and nights they'll lose
what's left of their reserves of glycogen
and die, having only ever processed
what was theirs from birth:
a pattern clenching against growth.
Almost obscured behind the field of light
the farmer knows that it was useless to call the vet.
So does the vet.
But there are some rituals
that must be carried through.

2. Erysipelas

The farmer and his rifle lean quietly on the rails.
Too late for penicillin.
The Ag Department notice put paid to that.
He should have acted earlier.
He thinks he even knows the one who brought it in,
the old Yorkshire boar he picked up at a clearing sale.
Not that it matters now.
The pigs are vomiting, if they feed at all,
and on their skin
are spreading reddish-purple wrinkled shapes.
Each day a little more.
The farmer thinks half consciously
they've turned into salamis before their time.
The image of a supermarket deli passes through his mind,
a range of processed pigmeats,
their piggy colours whole or sliced, bare or wrapped
laid out on plastic trays behind the glass,
all of it so cold and clean.
He leans on the rails,
which like everything else will have to be burnt.
He stabs with a boot
into the dirt, which will have to be treated.
Over at the house the rest of the family
is wondering if they'll have to leave.
It's getting late.
Loading the rifle for the first of many times
he wipes the bullet through his hair,
a habit handed down by his father,
who always oiled a bullet or a nail that way
before he banged it in.

3. Swine Dysentery

The pigs are feverish.
They're shitting stuff that looks like porridge
flecked with blood.
The pens are full of it.
The farmer bends down
and carefully looks at what's collected on his boots.
His fear is that the texture there
is bits of lining from the animals' intestines:
an appetite consuming itself.
If dysentery has gone that far
a farmer might as well just give the fight away.
But here it's not so bad, only a skirmish.
He thinks about what happened
to his father in the First World War,
that line the Sergeant was reported to have said
not long before the end,
You really know you've had it when you shit your guts out
and how the final letter home
described the colours of the war.
It said his father hardly ever saw blood red
because the colours were mostly dull:
drab uniforms, rank stews,
and when the glossy liquids in a man spilled out
they nearly always got mixed in with the mud.
Like someone planting seeds,
a man who hopes to start again after tragedy,
the farmer makes his way along the churned-up troughs
pushing in the pills of penicillin.
By the time he finishes
there's still a generous handful of the pills
left over in the box.
When he thinks how much his pigs are worth
these little powdery pearls cost bugger all.

Cheap enough to waste on pigs,
he says to himself as he walks away
thinking about that family of drugs
that might have saved his father.

The Farmer

He starts each day before it is a day,
the little kitchen spreading buttered light
across the yard while he stokes up the stove
and warms his pot of porridge on the hotplate.

Sustained by this for six or seven hours
he sets off down the lane with his two dogs,
a silent trio who know their way so well
the pre-dawn darkness doesn't mean a thing,

and when they come to where the heavy cows
are either sleeping randomly apart
or standing crowded up against the gate
the dogs run out in wide opposing arcs.

The farmer knows this herd so thoroughly
he doesn't have to keep a record book.
It's all in his head: the details of each cow,
from butterfat to who her mother was,

her temperament, what sicknesses she had,
the sort of calf she'd been, how well she does
on each particular type of feed, etc.
No need to write it down. It's what he is.

From there the cows move slowly, drugged with milk,
while the farmer and his dogs follow behind,
and by the time they reach the milking shed
it's light enough to see what's always there.

At the Sheep-parasite Field Day

In a paddock at the edge of town,
surrounded by cars and drought,
the international chemical firms
have got their latest products out

on trestle-tables and bales of hay
in a giant army-surplus tent.
The various tins of dip and spray,
standing in rows or stacked in pyramids,

are painted with colours that children would like
and printed with warnings
against allowing the contents onto your skin
or breathing the vapours in.

Most of the firms have German-sounding names,
and one of them we know
made the gas for the extermination camps
a few name changes ago.

Above an unattended display
an Ag Department video
is showing the recommended way
to dip a mob for lice and blowflies.

The sheep is forced into a sunken race
half-full of frothy liquid,
and when it lifts its face
the farmer standing on the side

uses a long pole
to make the animal completely disappear,
and with a further stroke pushes it backward
to open up the wool.

His action is the same
as one you sometimes see in Venice

when they're playing the tourist game,
gliding gondolas down poisoned canals.

Beside the video a poster shows in black and white
a handful of maggots
spread out on a dark surface
seen through a telescopic rifle sight.

In their pale shape
and in the random pattern they make
they're not unlike a mob of sheep
looked down on from an aeroplane.

The other part of this display,
the so-called infected specimen,
a ram with lice and pizzle strike,
is standing in a small pen

while two boys poke at him through the rails
with their ice-cream sticks.
Outside, more children are playing
among the cars and spare bales,

a kelpie chained up in a ute
is giving voice to her excitement,
and half a dozen brightly coloured brand-name flags
are rippling on top of the enormous tent.

It could almost be a circus
if it weren't so serious.

The Verandah

On still days you can hear the rifle range
five miles away, a crack now and then
in the brittle heat where the only other sound
is a faint but insistent fizz of cicadas.

It's not that hard to imagine what's happening
down there at the range. Things would be
pretty much the same as they were the last time
you dropped in, with your rifle and Esky.

Most of the men would be standing in front
of the clubrooms, holding their stubbies of VB,
talking amongst themselves while their rifles
and ammo were still on the back seats of their cars.

Only a few prone bodies would be out
at the 400-yard mark, motionless and facing
the giant embankment with its symbol tabs
arrayed on top like an old-fashioned cash register.

Each time a shooter has finished a bracket
the boy on the other side, bored, doing it
for beer-and-cigarette money, will pull down
a new constellation and phone through the score.

It's money for next to nothing. Between brackets
he just sits there reading a Phantom comic,
turning the pages as hesitantly then briskly
as they might be turned by a small breeze.

At home his mother sits in the kitchen
watching a fly on the table wander across
from bread crumbs to a drop of milk. It's mid-
afternoon and these moments are as slow as honey.

Sport

It has a narrative that gets you in,
a kind of play in which the final score
casts every move into its proper light;
and whether it's re-run on giant screens
that frown like Cyclops high above the grounds
or in the black-and-white consistencies
of Monday morning's double sporting spread
the big effect will always be the same –
some disappointment that the moment passed
without a chance to see it as it was,
not covered up with television lights
and ghastly logos from the corporate set
but naked human spirit on the line,
belief in self, backing your own judgment
into a place where all those warm-up rounds
are merely distant pointers to the form
that brought you to these instant memories
of being alone surrounded by a crowd,
maybe a hundred thousand rowdy fans
who want something that's lacking in themselves,
and seeing forward moves where truth is made
just boiling down to reflexes and luck ·
though in another sort of rational world
where sport might be a substitute for war
top squads would be selected from the ranks
of those who hate the system anyway
and budding solo players on the make
would be required to play their game in teams
thus making sure that countries like our own
could not exploit the re-run final scores
in ways that politicians seem to like,
and bringing back the basics of a style
that would unite the body and the mind,
a world where sport's true subject was itself.

The Practice Nets

The way a dream of sporting glory dissolves
when early morning light seeps grimly back
into the room, so too this half-constructed aviary
with its slabs of wire mesh and concrete floor.
Instead of dirty Tipp-Ex worms the droppings
are red-raw skid marks mostly in the middle
where some of the unhelmeted batsmen lost sight
of just the ball they needed to keep an eye on.
Their bats are like the pitch in miniature.
Each one is badly scarred with the hot spots
and rashes of that disease which spreads beyond
the playing victims to their wives and kids –
the sempiternal pain of a middle-order collapse.
But perhaps worse are those more personal wounds:
the split webbing after a dropped slips catch,
two broken toes from practising in sandshoes,
and everyman's nightmare of turning full-on
to an awkward ball without the vital box.
When banishment from next week's team is likely
the anatiferous number-three will come back
to this uncovered nave and go through strokes
with all the devotion of a former sinner.
Watching the one who used to be their idol
groups of schoolchildren will hang along the aisles,
their fingers poking dangerously through the wire.
An act of public penitence is always fraught.
The padded man who finds himself exposed
to such a swaying congregation is never sure
which ball is going to cut sharply off the seam.
The only choice is to practise a straight bat
as if the life of chance could be theorized.
Not that these children pushing against wire
would ever be impressed with a return to form
which only happened before the five real days.

They know that that's the attraction of the nets.
It doesn't matter how many times you're out.
You'll always carry your bat. It's like a dream.

So-and-so's Famous Poem

He probably just started with a single line,
some loose thread he hardly remembered picking up
on the edge of an uneventful afternoon.
It wouldn't have meant much to him on its own,
lying there without a context among his thoughts,
but even so there'd be no doubting its quirkiness.
On any wander through his big Collected Poems
that line still clings to you with its unexpectedness,
its atypical repose, saying at last the poet has relaxed.
The next few lines may well have been the same:
off-cuts, false starts and other by-products of his work
just thrown together to see how they looked.
It must have been luck, as much as anything else,
which made that opening part turn out the way it did:
four separate statements, each one quite bold
but not as disconnected as they first appear to be.
And perhaps it was here, with chance on his side,
he first arrived at the poem's exquisite form,
an enfolding of the old with the naturally new.
He would then have concentrated more on craft,
removing the slackness from each of the lines
and tying tight knots of rhyme at each second end.
By now he would have seen enough of the poem's shape
to know what sort of tension he was looking for
and teasing out new lines would be a bit easier.
The feeling of making something from almost nothing
should have been behind him and the poem's length
helping him along, one tied line suggesting another.
At this sweet point, with the fabric coming evenly together,
he might have wondered what the poem really was.
A love letter, an epitaph, or maybe a suicide note?
And if so, for whom was all the effort intended?
The obvious answer was that none of this mattered
and he would have got straight on with the job,
arranging his material with as much slow care

as a weaver working all day in front of a loom.
The further he went the more the poem would have
written itself, the pattern unfurling before him
until he would hardly have thought the poem his own.
He may even have felt the thing was commissioned
but he couldn't have said why or by whom.
It was like worship: these weren't the right questions.
The final lines, when they came, would have held
no surprise, as though they were already there
just waiting to be picked up by someone at hand.
And afterwards he would have been left with
a beautiful object, perfectly useless of course
but something to take to the grave, to anyone's grave.

Getting Through a Strained Fence

Approach it as you would a work of art.
Relax. Just be yourself. Then you can start
to see the fence for what it really is –
not some correctness test, an entry quiz
that leaves you wiping culture off your face –
but standard lines held truly in their place
by grey-box posts plugged into common ground.
Don't worry that the highest line is crowned
with barbs to stop you going over it,
they're only there so people will submit
themselves to bending down when getting through –
like daily prayer, the humble thing to do.
Indeed you wouldn't think a fence like this
was worth it if you didn't have to miss
at least a couple of the seven deadly sins.
The life of penitence often begins
this way. By bending underneath your pride
the change is more than just a change of side.
The most effective way of getting there
is with an awkward almost-roll. Prepare
yourself by turning sideways to the lines,
then stick your left leg out so it aligns
with them just slightly lower than your waist.
You'll notice that they're all precisely spaced
and that the gaps don't look like they'd expand.
But if you take the middle lines in hand
and use your other leg as one linchpin
you'll squeeze your horizontal body in
between the curving contours that you've formed.
Just there you might appear a bit deformed
caught up and bent forward like someone hurt,
and forced uncomfortably to face the dirt
for what will seem a drawn-out length of time,
though that passes as soon as you can climb
out through the gap and stand up straight again,

unfolding in an instant to regain
the balance that your body put aside.
From that moment you're on the other side.
A whole new paddock opens up its realms
of greener grass, the prospect overwhelms
you with its possibilities, and while
you fold your arms and try to reconcile
the future with the past, the present fence
still stands behind you making perfect sense.

The Calling of Saint Matthew

Only Caravaggio could have painted this room.
Everything about its narrative is questioning
the way a painting should look, pointing
out new beliefs for the problems that face
an artist when he or she first lays eyes
on a thing in its unformed mental light.

Unlike the written line it is now the light,
not Christ, which summons from beyond the room
and reaches long intensity in Levi's eyes.
For the first time in his life he is questioning
his life, having just come face to face
with his Lord who stands there pointing

languidly at him. Levi, surprised, is pointing
at himself – 'You mean me?' The light
is like an answer staring him in the face,
making it obvious that there is no room
here for further hesitating or questioning.
While he and his friends have raised their eyes

the two on his right have kept their eyes
on the table. One seems to have been pointing
at the money there, perhaps questioning
an amount. Like Holbein's gamblers the light
has shown them nothing new in the room.
They've missed their chance. The only face

they're interested in is the stern face
on a Roman coin reflected in their eyes.
But Levi's friends, in the middle of the room,
are both curious. Saint Peter is pointing
firmly at the one in the nearest light
who has leaned forward as if questioning

this intrusion. The other is also questioning
though not with the same aggression. His face
is turned to catch the high window light
and like Levi he is looking into Christ's eyes.
Despite all these figures looking and pointing
at each other nothing yet happens in the room.

But soon, without questioning, Levi will leave this room
and face the challenge that was pointing
at him. And the light will stay in his eyes.

Carracci's Self-portrait

There's nothing for the critics to explain,
no influence they could identify.
The painter's portrait is its own refrain –

you see the man and then see him again.
Two times but once he looks you in the eye.
There's nothing for the critics to explain.

Though some have tried it's always been in vain.
There isn't any theory to say why
the painter's portrait is its own refrain:

it's not a code. The canvases contain
two different questions but the same reply.
There's nothing for the critics to explain

because Carracci held them in disdain.
He knew the way they'd try to falsify
the painter's portrait. 'Is its own refrain

too smart by half?' they'd say. And they'd complain
it was impossible to justify.
There's nothing for the critics to explain.
The painter's portrait is its own refrain.

The Puddle

(El Pozo, *Jacinto Fombona Pachano*)

On bare soil, behind a mudbrick house,
the last of the afternoon rain
has come together in a clear puddle

where a child disperses navies
made of paper, twigs and illusions
in a pattern as original

as the response of sky above him
where stars and blatant clouds
detain themselves in passing

and this last afternoon of May
can see itself glimmering
in a fixed crystalline point.

Above a rubbish dump noisy birds
are swirling and colliding
like bits of blown plastic

and where the breeze serenely blows
it brings with it the stories
of those crowded hills.

Everywhere the eye turns
there is another view of misery
more freighted than the last:

scattered families come together
for the funeral of a child,
a mother begs for food

and from the rotting heaps
and warm ground a thin steam rises
to form tomorrow's tears.

But before tomorrow turns
a fiery morning sun will look
into the abandoned puddle,

and as its glare increases
the clear stillness will be blinded
and completely emptied of expression.

Saint Francis and the Angels

It used to be said that they were cities
of the future, that in the next new age
they'd be seen as the first of their sort:
beacons on the West Coast, their light spreading
across cultures until highrises and freeways
were as common as kitsch Palladian copies.

But although a small country often copies
a big country it doesn't mean their cities
should look the same. Not everyone wants freeways
and other products of the American Age,
like rows of billboards, spreading
into their environment and minds. The sort

of countries that find it hard to sort
out this mess of who you are when copies
of someone else's culture are spreading
all over the place via your big cities
are those new countries of the Post-Colonial Age.
For them the future doesn't mean the freeways

of another country. It means the freeways
of Progress: a beautiful system to sort
and deliver new products from an age
that's best remembered for its copies of copies.
In fact, there's no reason that the cities
themselves can't be part of this way of spreading

the product. Aren't they made for spreading
as much as for containing? What are freeways
if not the trade routes of the cities
and they in turn just products of another sort?
It's an idea each new country copies
with vigour. They seem to be products of an age

whose philosophy is to develop but not to age.
There's no way you can stop it from spreading.
Momentum builds and the sheer number of copies
carries through until highrises and freeways
and billboards are found in every sort
of location worldwide even though the two cities

of an earlier age are no longer the best cities
to examine. They're still spreading a sort
of original but it's copies that jam the freeways.

The New Floor

Digging three rows of holes to start with
the remembrance of physical work comes early,
that moment of unguardedness when the load
is shared equally between body and mind,
something it has in common with palpable love:
a design feature to stop the species dying out.
Its symptoms are tentative beads of sweat,
a deeper breathing that falls into step,
and the sensation of having new hands,
of feeling them tighten with plump blood.
Waiting to be remembered after these fade
is the pleasure of knowing how things work
and a reminder of the ordinary details involved.
For instance, the simplicity of your tools:
hammer and nails, chisel, pencil and saw.
And for your measurements not much except
a spirit level and a roll of string.
No amount of big technology could make
the finished floor more level than these can.
It's as good as that other thing, poetry,
which only needs a pencil and some paper.
With love the lines fit into logics of their own:
the first of redgum stumps, then tin caps, bearers,
joists, and finally the bare pine boards.
They lie there at the end of low-tech work,
tongue in groove and side by side as tight
as lines from Dante's faithfully measured book:
an understanding to keep the years together.

Little Elegies

For children lost in accidents on farms
it's that much further for their parents' love.

Their grief, receding closer to their child,
begins with time and place, and random cause.

The fatal tractor grumbles down a lane
just like it did before the sway-bar slipped;

the shotgun leans off-duty in the shed,
its bright red cartridges like fallen fruit;

the dully sliding channel looks unmoved
by drama at the culvert yesterday;

and where the tiger-snake was killed too late
some tidy ants are picking meat from bones.

For those two people living with this death
the silent meals, the nights of lying still

are like it always is when they're apart.
At any time it seems that one of them

has stopped half-way through packing little clothes
into a box and stands there loose with tears

while in a distant paddock in the heat
the other one is shovelling out a drain,

becoming more and more obsessed with work:
as though they might as well have never met.

The Garden

There'll never be a better time to die,
not with the garden looking so alive.
See how that iris focuses the eye
on filmy purple dabs, how they contrive

to keep attention on themselves when all
around them other flowers are crying out
in colours just as pure; a visual call
that ranges from a whisper to a shout.

The beds will never be like that again:
long moments of excess not knowing how
the crumbling dirt is going to sustain
you any more. The dying time is now.

The Prey

The praying mantis keeps as green and still
as the flowering basil stalk on which he's poised.
Around him in the garden a cabbage moth

digresses unpredictably the way they do.
At length, and not without a few false landings
where the moth would seem to settle on a plant

only to fling itself into the air again,
it perches on the seed-head of the stalk
and starts to nibble at the small white flowers.

Confirmed in his disguise and calm crouched wait
the mantis re-adjusts his deltoid head
and slowly starts to stalk along the stalk,

two fishingline-like feelers cast out in front.
The moth is very quick at seeing things
above it such as insect-eating birds

but has poor sight for danger rising underneath.
The first and last it knows about the mantis
is when two hooked and levered forelegs snatch

it into extended jaws with trap-snap speed.
Clamped hard against the feeding face there is
no struggle. The frail white wings, one at a time,

spin down like petals falling off a flower
and the praying mantis keeps as green and still
as the flowering basil stalk on which he's poised.

Leaving

She left the hospital quietly at night.
The lights were out and only a skeleton staff
remained in the office on her first-floor ward.

Outside the streets were dark with drizzle
and there were only a few cars around,
making a smooth tearing sound as they passed.

She noticed that the cars were very old, pre-war,
but were shining in good condition anyway
and that the city centre had a human scale,

the sort of scale it used to have when she
first came here with her parents sixty years ago.
The highest objects were the crosses on the spires.

By the time she reached the station the sun was up
and the platform was a rather frightening place
with its cross-currents of adults dressed for work.

A train had just arrived and from its van
men in overalls were unloading wooden crates.
She held her mother's hand as she'd been told to.

The station building hadn't changed a bit.
Its famous row of clocks under the copper dome,
its tiled floors and timber ceilings were all intact.

Moving off, the train whistled and she saw again
the enamel platform sign, cast-iron framed,
which had cast her mind's image of that number.

It only took a few suburbs before the train
was out in a landscape of fifty-acre farms
where harnessed horses and small grey tractors

both worked the paddocks, and where the roads,
even the main ones back to town, weren't sealed.
Sometimes she saw a farmer waving at the train.

Her carriage creaked and swayed like an old bed.
It seemed to her the further away they went
the more she recognized the farms and little towns.

The home stop, when it came, was feverishly hot
and the light was very harsh. She squinted
with interest at the lack of progress in this town.

It was here as a girl she had first seen life
away from the formality of her parents' farm.
Nothing since had been as new as that look.

The station was as crowded as it had been then.
Most of the population seemed to be there
for it was the railway that kept the town alive.

Soon the train began to take on new passengers.
She waited until she had to give up her place
and then stepped out into the terrible light.

A Memorial Service

Emerging from the little church
those muted fifties suits
and wonder-fabric dresses

seem just as sad and lifeless
as when they're hanging up
in varnished plywood cupboards

between weddings and funerals
for six months at a stretch –
those crosses on the calendars.

Outside it's past a hundred
and every steering wheel
is too hot to hold.

The farmers and their wives
at first bunch up as tight
as suits and dresses on a rack

to say the same familiar things
to the widow standing there
with children at her side

and then spread slowly out
the way that cows do
when let into a fresh paddock.

There's beer and lemonade
laid out on trestle-tables
in the shade of big redgums

but most of the congregation
is still thinking about
the details of the eulogy,

a list of main events,
both self-imposed and not,
so common they seem clichéd

to those from somewhere else
but which are real enough
for anyone involved with them:

an isolated station childhood,
impulsive under-age enlistment,
imprisonment in Palestine,

a soldier settlement block,
and then the growing parallels
of family and farm

until the common pulse
gave out in a bright room
cluttered with technology.

It makes them think about
their own peculiar list,
how ordinary it would seem

set out on one short slab
of main points and praise
as final as a headstone,

how everything left out
would be as hackneyed
as the flesh off the bone.

Abandoning the main body
a little at a time,
mostly in long-time pairs,

they walk back to their cars
and talk of getting out of
these best clothes at last.

The Pier

Upset about death you go for a walk
and finish up down at the pier
watching the old men with their long rods

that doodle slowly like distraction.
It's overcast and out there on the bay
squalls are circling like seagulls.

The pier runs a hundred metres into the sea
and you notice that the beams
of Oregon or whatever across the top of it

are weathered as blunt at their ends
as the fingers of those fishermen
and that the big wooden thumbs

where a ship would be tied up
are neatly capped with bird-droppings.
Each time a wave crashes along underneath

there is the rickety sound of train travel
and the two rows of tree trunks
supporting and extending the platform

are worn away a little bit more.
Above the waterline they look complete
but when that line breathes down

it's worrying to see how much
the lower parts have been decayed away
and you imagine it all collapsing in the future.

The further out you go the more
those trunks have been weakened
in the place they most need to be secure

and the deeper the water looks
(so deep it's hard to figure out
just how they would have built the pier)

until on a plank made slippery
with scales and fishgut stains and seaspray
you come to the end.

From *Things Happen*

A Jillaroo

She's driving through the back country night,
her moleskins moony pale in the dashboard light,

her kelpie asleep on the passenger-side floor,
his head only inches from the gravel roar,

and on the back seat a copy of *The Bulletin*
and her dirty work clothes, scented with lanolin.

Turning onto bitumen her headlights sweep
the low-star eyes of a paddockful of sheep,

a row of fence posts' barely functional geometry
and the very slow explosion of a gum tree.

Settling into the sealed road's quieter hum
she thinks back over the distance she's come

in one day through saltbush plains and small towns
from her rough apprenticeship at Yanko Downs,

how this morning's paddocks had a frosty glow,
which nearly doubled how far a cooee could go,

how last week she'd seen two half-cut jackeroos
fire their shotguns into a flock of cockatoos,

and how the Queensland shearers all went home
when the boss cocky tried to bring in the wide comb.

A few miles down the road she notices the big
expensive light-show of a tractor and rig

pulling far out on the horizon like a ship.
It turns towards her then disappears into a dip.

She looks back in time to dodge a kangaroo
looming fast like a drunk at a woolshed do.

The Meaning

Last night a pair of eyes
shone back at me
when I poked the torch out
the side door to see

what had made the dog
go off like a crude alarm,
echoing his urgency
across the still farm;

a pair of eyes
over near the chook shed,
low down, close together
and like Mars, faintly red.

Probably a neighbour's cat,
or a feral one,
its guts full of all
the damage it had done.

I told the dog to shut up
like you would a child
and went back to bed
where the doona was piled

roughly at the bottom
with the sheet,
a big sack of feathers
losing my body heat.

This morning at first light,
with a heavy frost
sheeting on the ground,
I counted the cost

of my mistake –
our six chooks dead
and scattered in bits
in their corrugated shed.

It looked as if there'd been
a pillow fight
that got out of hand:
blood on the white

feathers, dead eyes open
and astonished, legs
bitten off, and the remains
of broken eggs.

I happened to look up
and saw a fox
running away through
the white far paddocks.

It ferreted across
the grass's frozen quilt
with enough speed
to resemble guilt,

a wriggling blip
on the monochrome
of a large computer screen.
Heading back home

it stopped once,
and turned and scanned
this farm, as if blood
were the meaning of the land.

Bucolica

'A paddock is a poem,' wrote the man,
'Each paddock has its own peculiar form.
With paddocks, as with art, there is no norm
You comprehend a paddock when you can.'

'A poem is a paddock,' wrote the man,
'You put down lines like fences when you start
And try to strain them into works of art.
The posts are measured so the fence will scan.'

'A poem, like a paddock, is a space.
A paddock, like a poem, is a lie.
I gauge myself in both of them and try
To show that each one is the other place.'

The Land Itself

Beyond all arguments there is the land itself,
drying out and cracking at the end of summer
like a vast badly-made ceramic, uneven and powdery,
losing its topsoil and its insect-bodied grass seeds
to the wind's dusty perfumes, that sense of the land,
then soaking up soil-darkening rains and filling out
with the force of renewal at the savoured winter break.
Sheep and cattle are there with their hard split feet.
They loosen topsoils that will wash away or blow away,
punishing the land for being so old and delicate,
and they make walking tracks that run like scars
across the bitten-down paddocks stitched with fences
while the farmers in their cracked and dried-out boots
wait for one good season to make their money green again.
In places where the land has begun to heal itself
there are the younger old cuisines, softer footed,
the emu farms and kangaroo farms, both high-fenced
and nurtured by smart restaurants and tax write-offs.
Further out where the colours are all sun-damaged
and the land is sparse and barely held together
you find the future waiting for its many names.
Company personnel in mobile labs are already there,
taking readings and bouncing lumps of jargon off satellites.
A field geologist sits in an air-conditioned caravan.
She sees in front of her a computer screen of numbers
then through a dust-filtered window the land itself.
She looks back and forth. Something here is unrealized.
It might be an asset. It might be an idea.

A House in the Country

The first we knew about this hidden force
was when a crack appeared in the masonite
outside the children's bedroom, starting from
up under one end of the windowsill
and taking a jagged diagonal course
that led down to the bottom of the wall
as if it were a chart of our bad luck.

With burglar care I used a jemmy to pry
the two large pieces of this puzzle off
their web-filled grid of noggins and studs
and saw immediately the tell-tale dry
mud tubes that were plastered to several of
the concrete stumps, those conduits termites make
to get out of the earth and into the goods.

The first stud I prodded buckled and split
and something hard to focus on, a sprinkling
of tiny cloned albino movement, split
and dispersed, and was followed by even more
when I levered the stud apart, the panic of
a light-shy mass, so translucently pale
they looked as if they weren't fully formed.

Again I rowed the jemmy through a stud
and got the same result, more spillage
from what was now no longer a closed circuit,
and with a teenage vandal's feeling of
futility and despair I smashed the mud
conduits on the stumps within my reach,
releasing a more concentrated flow.

I gazed at this miniature apocalypse
of countless termites writhing in exposure,
no doubt programmed to crave the opposite
of Goethe, who had cried *More light! More light!*

and as the seconds dropped away as small
and uniform as termites a feeling burrowed
into me as bad as if I had cancer.

I thought about the treatment this would mean:
those poisons, vile as chemotherapy,
that they'd have to spray all round the place,
a pile of new timber, tin caps between
the bearers and the stumps, and hours, maybe days
spent wandering the paddocks like prospectors
on the off-chance that we'd find the nest.

Somewhere out there, sealed in a slightly warm
and humid city was the bloated queen,
unable to move, surrounded by her swarm
of attendants, an evil sausage producing more
and more termites that would eat our home.
I set off at a fast walk, worried about
what was going on underneath my feet.

A Decaying Form

This afternoon, walking along the creek,
I found the bleached shell of a freshwater tortoise
sitting upright on the bank,
as wide and white
as a dinner plate.
It had the pleasing smooth convexity of a mushroom
but when I picked it up and went knock knock
anyone home
the hardness was more like something fossilized.

The domic top was engraved with a neat pattern
of about a dozen
soft-cornered rectangles, two in the centre
and the rest around them petal fashion
spreading to the edge.
Set into each of these was a myriad
of tiny interlocking ruptured kidney shapes similar
to the jigsaw on the outside
of a model of the human brain.
All this detail was now in bad
condition thanks to the wind and sun.

The plate
underneath
was smooth
and flat,
faint
brown,
more
square
than
round.

It was connected to the top part of the shell
by curvy front, back and side pillars
that had also begun to decay

and looked quite ornamental
in an Art Nouveau sort of style,
along the lines of Gaudi.
The gaps these flared supports created
stared out at me like the eye sockets of a skull.

Peering in,
the way you'd hold binoculars,
at the stale-smelling interior
I saw an incomplete line
of minute knuckles clinging along the centre
of the bulging ceiling –
the last remains of this defensive creature's backbone.
I reached in and ran my finger down
the fragile zipper.
All of them spilled away except one,
which stayed there
dangling like a trinket.

Dissatisfied as a child
who's broken something it doesn't understand
I frisbeed
the shell into the creek thinking that
would be the end of it
but Hattie, always ready for some sport,
plunged in and grabbed
the thing and brought
it back and dropped it at my feet,
as if this were only the beginning.

The Drinkers

All around the dam, sentry spaced,
are clumps of bitten-down and dried-out rushes:
bristling, defensively braced
echidnas in colour, size and shape.

They flourished outrageous spiky hairdos
that would pierce your skin,
which worked until
three hungry white goats were let in.

Now dozens of bees are drinking at the edge
of this relative ocean.
They hover up and down
like particles of energy bouncing in slow motion

and then all at once are dispersed
when Hattie wanders through them
unaware and contented
on her way to have a swim.

She forges out in a straight line, stops
and continues round and round
like a rudder-jammed boat,
drinking as she goes with a slurpy clopping sound.

Emerging on the farther shore
with her black pelt sleek with wet weight
she gives herself a staggering shake
that manages momentarily to imitate

the size of a peacock's raised display –
a water-drop composite fan
is thrown up, tinted by the sun
and drops away.

The curious goats come down for a drink as well,
chewing their cud.
They sink down closer to themselves
as their front legs make pole holes in the mud.

One goat lifts her stumpy tail to eliminate
a jackpot of black pellets,
which Hattie comes to investigate,
nodding while sniffing, as if making a count.

Across the other side, in the shallows,
each time breasting an instant ring of water,
two curvy swallows
are swooping down to scoop up tiny beakfuls.

Later, when the sunlight fails
kangaroos will have their turn,
sliding at the final muddy stage on temporary skis
and anchoring themselves with muscly tails.

Midday Horizon

The summer's worn-out paddocks
aligned as neatly as quatrains on a page,
one of those highly buffed duco skies,
and in between, a fine graph line
as nervy as a lot of black snakes in the heat.
Great sheets of mirage are lying there
as bright as new galvo.
You squint into the glare until your eyes
are nothing more than two short twitching lines
and see on the horizon
the standing shadow of a eucalyptus tree.
A big mob of sheep is moving to the left,
breaking up and catching up
in slow eddies like a lava flow.
Seen through the hot distorting air
clear flames seem to be tearing off the mob.
A man is walking sheep-slow behind them.
From where you are
his shape is continually being modified
as if he were walking through different dimensions.
Sometimes he seems to slip into separate pieces,
then pull back together, temporarily.
The same thing is happening to the tree.
The man stops
and a low piece of him draws right away this time.
It must be a dog.
You notice the silence, how near it is.
There's no threat that you can see
and yet the thin exposed horizon trembles.

The Snake in the Department Store

Two farm boys riding bikes along a track
come rolling to a stop when up ahead
a ripple of the loose dirt seems to move.
They watch the brown snake cast a wavy tread

no wider than the lines their bike tyres make
and then instinctively they drop their bikes
together like a bingle, rush the snake
and pin his angry head down with a stick.

The body flings itself around as much
as what is pinning it keeps straight and still.
For several minutes, while a bike wheel spins,
these different four-foot lengths compete until

an end is plucked out of the movement
and the snake is hoisted into straining air.
Unsure of what to do with such a prize
the boy not holding it suggests a dare.

His day-pack is unzipped and emptied out,
then cautiously the snake is lowered in,
the stick is used again and soon withdrawn
and the zipper quickly given back its grin.

With motion going nowhere in their pack
the two boys pedal five miles into town,
debating how and where this slippery jack
might possibly be let out of his box.

The town is quiet on a Wednesday.
Outside the PATTERSON'S DEPARTMENT STORE
a ute is parked with half a dozen sheep,
one fly-struck, wafting farm smells through the door.

The boys decide that this looks like the spot
for their experiment, and saunter in

to find themselves in FURNITURE. The squat
puffed shapes of bargain lounge suites crowd the room.

Two ladies dressed in floral patterns, both
of which would look at home on cushions, stand
examining a striped reclining chair.
One lady has a brochure in her hand.

The boys, pretending to be interested
in something nearby, set the day-pack on
a sofa, pull the zipper back enough
and wander over to an Aubusson-

style carpet crafted in the Philippines.
The snake comes oozing through the daylight slit
and disappears beneath the sofa's bulk.
Nothing happens for a while, then it

emerges from the other side and slides
behind the unobservant ladies, goes
between a pair of chairs and out of sight
again. It's gone. Then suddenly it flows

serenely down the aisle and through the door.
The boys arrive to see it cross behind
the man returning to his ute and pour
like dirty water after summer rain

into a gutter grate. They stand there on
the footpath while the man backs out his flock
and feel that since the snake was never seen
the whole affair has somehow been a flop.

Woman with an Axe

She sits on the splitting-block
in the middle of the afternoon,
leaning over her upturned axe

with one hand round the handle's neck,
the way someone else
might sit on a kitchen chair

at the end of a summer day
and strum a few slow chords
on a relaxed guitar.

An axestone fits into her other hand
coldly and firmly,
like a small coarse discus.

It makes a fine grinding sound
monotonous as flies,
in little insistent circles

like a killer killing time,
as it focuses the shiny edge
into an evil smile.

Up and down the nearby trunk
of a lemon-scented gum
a grey fantail moves from one

minute meal to another,
jabbing and then accelerating on
with shuttlecock speed.

The woman watches as if
listening to a faraway sound,
then tests the sharpened edge

gently, with her thumb,
the way you'd tease
a soft note from a guitar.

She looks at the green wood
laid out in front of her,
three new logs of red gum,

one still slowly shedding the hard tears
of its translucent colour
from a miraculous site,

and thinks how she'll chop
a length or two
for the primal pleasure it gives:

the knock of the swung head
impacting through the packed fibre,
the shock of it

rocketing back up the handle,
and the chips spinning off
to land in the grass.

Already she can smell
the resinous freshness
of the dry chiselled vee.

Close behind her,
up against the paling fence,
the sawn blocks of grey box

are stacked on their sides
with cellar neatness
in an insecure pyramid.

Each block on its end,
when struck with the axe,
will split in its own way.

Some will burst into halves
almost too easily,
as if spring-loaded.

Others will tear unwillingly
down the grain, and hang
together in a splintery embrace.

And one, there is always one,
will bounce the axe
like metal meeting metal.

She puts down her tools
and looks to their weatherboard house
where a slight rupture of smoke

is drilling straight up
from the pitted orange-brick chimney
of their wood-fire stove

that has burned continuously
since the First War,
if her mother is to be believed.

The Exploding Snake

The red-bellied black snake
lies on the bitumen road
in the morning sunshine,
warming his load
of instinctive blood.

To him the road is a big rock
and he lies along it
pointing the same route,
a black line among
white ones, taking stock
of the world
with his lively tongue.

The warmth of the road
rises into him
and he receives it
like a subtly vibrating code.
When those messages grow coarse
with something other than heat
he draws away from their source.

But not quickly enough of course.
The truck wheel rolls over his length in an instant,
rushing most of his blood
to his head,
which bursts with such force
it sounds like a bullet
going off in a campfire.
Can't be the snake!
The driver steps on the brake
Convinced he's blown a tyre.

Nocturnal

On summer nights,
when moonlight cools the air
and Mr Fox, the nosey one,
is checking chooksheds on his rounds,

when half the flowers
have clenched their colours out of sight
and nearly all the birds
are fixed and comatose,

that's when the roos appear,
drawn in from desiccated paddocks by our lawn,
a watered smaller paddock that provokes
their curiosity and appetite.

Among the monochromes and bushy blurs
their shapes possess a cut-out clarity,
tipping up then down
with silhouette puppet simplicity.

Their work is mostly routine
as a bureaucrat's,
straightforward head-down stuff
involving little areas of grass,

though sometimes when they get bored
they scratch a flower bed
and leave the bulbs exposed
like archaeology

or nip a gum-tree seedling off
an inch above the ground
and bite the small trunk into segments
as neat as something on a chopping board.

Once, when there were two big males
I saw them start to fight

beside the loquat tree,
two shadows mirrored by attack.

They scratched and bit
in an exaggeration of the way
that furry partners check
each other for a flea,

the dead weight of their tails
now curved to form a powerful spring
that pushed them into range
of pointed swipes.

Standing near the house
in bare feet on the dewy grass
I watched them lunge
repeatedly while all the female roos

just grazed the lawn,
not taking any notice of these two
who scuffled for the chance
to enter variations on a line.

Two Dogs

The smell of fox is as strong as burnt hair.
Even my nose knows there's something there.

For Hattie's twitching snout it must be overload.
She eyes the thick coffee bushes beside the road

then crashes in and disappears from sight
though not from sound. I wait for the fight

to begin but all that happens is first one bush,
then others lurch as if given a sudden push.

Eventually a gingered fox steps out near me
and lopes away across the paddock casually

with Hattie following in a natural contrast,
running much more energetically but not as fast.

The further they go, these dogs, one wild, one tame,
the more obvious it is which has won the game.

The student keeps on losing ground to the master.
And gives up. Wild things are always faster.

Those Yabbies

All that day the bulldozer ground back and forth
with a pendulum's arc in the widening hole.
Fixed as a boxer with one straight punch
it produced surfaces and low battlements
soon to be replaced by more copies of copies.
Its rhythm built hillocks at each end,
new highs and lows for fifty bucks an hour.
I loved the clean dirt, those gravels and clays.
At dusk the driver dropped to his feet
and became quaint down there in the vast middle,
having a piss. 'Well it's a start!' he yelled.
The dam lay before us, slung into the earth,
monstrous enough for the worst war crimes.

It filled in a few winter weeks once the rain
began to run like a rumour off the high ground
in the State Forest at the back of our place,
and in no time at all the holes appeared
like machine-gun spray above the waterline,
most of them large enough to fit your big toe.
And then there were claws and body shells
around the dam like broken discarded toys
and a single shag holding its wings pegged out
or tipping underwater with a splash as if yanked.
I first saw yabbies near the edge after dark,
in pairs, testing three elements. They torpedoed
backward out of the torch's bent barrel of light.

On land they were unnimble as the bulldozer
though their claws could still manage a dog's nose.
They kept sinking new holes, as if dissatisfied.
Enough of them could ruin a levee, my father said.
Where had they come from? For a while
I imagined them struggling overland at night,
drawn on by secret knowledge of the new dam.
But they were being airlifted there as eggs

by spoonbills, ibises and white-faced herons,
swinging in on the end of long pruned legs.
Later I saw the eggs, crimson and small as seeds,
packed in rows on a mother's sectioned underside,
her tail's three leaves folding nurture over them.

Squatting at the edge we threw that one back
but most we added to a bucket of slow wrestles.
They found it hard to give up the meated string
and would rise from the dam in a rescue scene
rather than let go. They'd slide from the bucket
still hanging on to each other in clumps
like models of uncommon molecular structures
and sink into the big boiling pot with a squeal
that was heated air escaping from their shells.
A bucketful would give you one good pile
of bleached pink nuggets steaming in a bowl.
We'd sprinkle salt and lemon juice and down them
with beer, as happy as the peasants we were.

The Creek

Boc! The empty tinnie
lands out there among
the glossy reproductions

of overhanging redgums,
takes a sip on them,
tips and sways upright

and glides into
the still cumbungi
like a modern swan.

Fst! Another tinnie
fizzes into life
with rabid foam.

Across the far side
a rusty forty-four
half-sunk in mud

is leaking something
out over the surface
with rainbow colours.

All things are aflowing
except that sheep carcass
snagged on something

upstream in the middle
where that distinctive smell
is coming from.

The tip of one horn
is poking through the surface
like another snag

and bright green shoots
of some sort of grass,
maybe wallaby grass,

are arising from
the sodden wool:
an odd reminder

of sprouting seeds
in cotton wool
a long time ago.

And look! Here comes
the water-rat,
unzipping the surface,

his little dark eyes
staring up at me
with bitterness.

The Incident Room

We're gathering information, different approaches,
heaping them up, trying them out.

We love what we're doing.
The risk. The sweat.

It seems like mindless work.
But something in it leads us sweetly on.

Glancing up I see the bare bulb's light
overwhelmed by afternoon.

Tactics, angles, clues present themselves.
But all we really have is our instinct.

Sometimes I feel we're close.
Sometimes I don't know what to think.

Her First Poem

She writes with patience
in a sloping spidery hand,
rephrasing each sentence
and trying out all sorts of tones.

Sometimes she uses rhyme and rhythm
when the lines seem incomplete:
a kind of homage
to the metred heart.

Occasionally
she watches short lines
falling casually
like Rilke's withered leaves.

And once, a style distracts her
where the poem is a joke
and words are proffered
for their own sake.

She works on through the afternoon
not noticing the clock hands
briefly becoming one,
scissoring together then apart,

but noticing that spider
writing out a new web
in the corner, its felt dark abdomen
tapered like a nib.

Outside her study window
freeway traffic
stretches and contracts
like slow elastic.

By evening there's a clean draft
on the page in front of her,

a kind of gift,
reminding her how someone

gave her cocaine
at a party years ago,
a short line,
laughing, 'Here, the first one's free!'

'Is that an Ulster accent I detect?'
I'm lying on the trolley like a specimen
beside the leucophoresis machine.
The nurse regards me for a moment then
answers cautiously, 'Yes, that's correct.'
I tell her I'm Australian though my genes,
or most of them, originate from there
and she tells me how long she's been out here.
The red lights on the panel flash as if
it's not long till a bomb somewhere goes off.
She takes a lumen and my catheter
then pushes slowly so the lines connect
and saline comes to me from the machine.
We trade the names of Northern Irish towns
and find our mothers' home towns are the same:
so while she works on me I chat with her
around the edges of a heritage.
I tell her how my parents came out here
by ship in fifty-one and that my father
still gets his home-town paper by airmail
and knows the goings-on in Joycean detail.
The nurse unpacks a needle and a line.
'We're probably related,' she almost jokes,
but wary of which side I'm on she looks
me in the eye, just momentarily,
a look that asks, 'Are your folks killing mine?'
The tourniquet is tightened to a grip
and veins rise up in long soft flexed protest.
I watch the needle hovering over me.
It's big. It goes in slowly and it hurts.
I watch the blood run through the line. It's fast.
The machine begins to pump. The pain gets worse.
I think of saying something but the vein bursts.
Inside my elbow it begins to spasm blue.
The machine shuts down and switches on a light.

The needle is withdrawn, the site bound tight.
The muscles in my arm begin to spasm too.
And then the blind convulsions spread
all through my body, carried there by blood.
The nurse tells me the name of this reaction
and fills a big syringe with valium,
undoes my catheter, makes a new connexion
and pushes in the calming drug. 'No harm,'
she says, in the accent of my childhood home,
and goes around to try the other arm.

Prognosis

This chemotherapy has humbled me.
It has a sickening simplicity.

I understood it from the first moment
it was given like a sacrament.

Next door the gripped unrhythmical noise
of someone dry retching continues.

The plastic sac of poison looms over my bed:
plump, sleek, like an organ that's been removed.

It drips at heartbeat pace down the line
along with valium and pethidine.

Next door the buzzer goes off like a heart attack.
Someone in a white coat goes to check.

There are too many words for my disease.
I know death is nothing after this.

Haematopoietics

The firmness of the desk has given
way to the cushioned uncertainty of
      the hospital bed.

The fountain pen and its sharp nib
have been exchanged for a syringe
      and a needle.

A sheet of ruled paper before me
has turned into an unwritten surface
      of sweating skin.

That page's pale blue straight lines
have curved and mingled, grown
      to different lengths

and sunk below the skin where they
are still visible and can be felt
      in tender places.

The thin black ink that flowed
whenever there was an opening has
      thickened to red.

And what is happening to me now?
Is this dark dot halfway up my arm
      the full stop

at the end of a death sentence,
or is it the only sign of something
      never written down,

something too painful even to say?

The Sick Poem

The poem has cancer.
You couldn't make it
look any worse
and feel any worse
if you threw acid
on the page afterwards.
It began as a minor complaint
and spread to be an obsession.
They say it has something
to do with words
but no-one really understands
how it works.
A well-paid team of experts
is looking through it,
a sample has been taken
and yes, words were there.
But what does that tell you?
There's a theory
if you ignore the thing
then it will go away
but all experience shows
it just keeps coming back
more and more.
Perhaps you should
love what's wrong with it?
Embrace the flaw:
a failure of communication,
an inability to form
the right words
at the appropriate time.
If this were something big,
say life or death,
there might be some insights
to be had from each stage,
like the hard wisdom

suffering is supposed to give you
but doesn't really.
Think of what goes on
in all those hospitals.
Perhaps the problem
is one of bad manners:
those clapped-out poeticisms
struggling across the page
through a damaged form.
I'm telling you straight:
to use a metaphor
at a time like this
would be obscene.

The Last Few Days and Nights

So weakened by life he could just pass
through the world this hospital bed,
he lies as still as someone already dead.
Hi-tech machines surround him now like family.

Three floors below him lies the mortuary.
People there have been cleaned of their identity.
Impossible to tell who wore the business suits,
the pilot's uniform or the comfortable shorts.

A nurse comes in to tend to the machines.
Reaching across him to one of them her breast,
the left one, is momentarily pressed
into his face with pillow-pressure softness.

He opens his eyes as if to some memory.
She gives him a look as intimate as surgery.

Home is Where the Hurt Is

These days I take my dying seriously,
after having tried, and failed, to make it into a joke.
The silence was what doomed me ultimately:
all those nervous attempts to provoke

a set response, anything to keep the flights
of fancy going no matter how insincere.
I was like an actor blinded by the footlights,
not sure if an audience is really there.

Now I'm living out the whole thing in my mind.
Not death itself, the overwhelming fact
of our existence, but that moment when we find
a link between our life and death, the final act.

Each connexion is lived through, then undone.
Happy. Sad. Sacred. Scared. Every day a different one.

Cytotoxic Rigor

A chemical spill in the body. You're still alive,
though the vein they ran it through won't survive.

You stiffen and shake. You give yourself emphasis.
There are tears in your eyes. There's blood in your piss.

The drugs they've added to tone down the shock
are as useless as the words from a prayer book.

A creature expands in your guts, in your being.
It squirms and it grabs. It has no meaning.

You vomit through surges of nausea and pain.
And when there's nothing left to vomit you vomit again.

More Light, More Light

Sickly sunlight through the closed curtains
that are white but much thicker than a sheet.
Sunlight with all the life taken out of it,
diminished but still there, an afterglow,
like the presence of a friend who has died.
You're lying still and yet you're moving fast.

A nurse comes in to give the drip a shot.
He opens the curtains in a moment of revelation.
The sunlight is revitalized into an opportunist
and instantly takes over the room like a brilliant virus,
filling out even the places you had never thought to look.
Your life is changed. The room is shown to you as it is,
not as it dimly appeared to you all that time ago.
You're moving fast and yet you're going nowhere.

Wordy Wordy
Numb Numb

Death.
Now there's a word.
He wrote it down.

It didn't take up much space.
You could say it was discreet,
and patient.

He couldn't remember
the first time he'd heard it.
It seemed to have been always there,

like something he owned
as a kind of right or inheritance.
But he wasn't sure if this was true.

He liked the way it rhymed
with breath,
its natural opposite.

He liked it for many reasons,
and because of that
he wrote it down many times

in many different contexts
finding that it had
all sorts of meanings.

Later on, when words had passed,
he backed it up
by dying.

One thing
he had always remembered
was the arrogance of health,

those dumb days
when nothing can touch you,
when death is just one

of the familiar short words:
sun, moon, tree, bread, wine, house, love...
you know them,

each one worn smooth
as a river stone
with the flow of language

and death the odd one out,
not so much worn smooth
as numb.

Better not to think about it then
and come back to it later
when it comes back to you

like an unpaid debt
gathering interest
infinitely greater than what was lent.

The Precise Moment

The surgeon cuts a green apple in half,
pressing down on the white plate until
two almost identical sections are revealed,

the little stem surviving intact on one
like a dark wick on a short fat candle.
The knife is not as sharp as he prefers

and instead of slicing through a pip
it has merely pushed it down and to one side,
leaving a curved burrow mark that might

have been made by a foul-tasting bug.
He picks up a half, noticing his hand,
his long fingers still smelling of antiseptic –

You'll be a pianist, his mother used to say –
and takes a bite that leaves a rough
and temporary record of his front teeth.

About to take a second bite he sees
a bit of brown badness and cuts it out
with the sort of precision you'd expect:

the dull knife, his hand and wrist combining
in a movement as routine as turning
a key in a lock. It's over in a moment.

He remembers this morning, cutting that flesh,
the first incision a line drawn through softness,
it widened and filled with wine-dark blood.

The lights were brighter than this light;
the knife was smaller, sharper and shinier;
the hands were cleaner. Did he get it all?

He notices a slight brown film already gathering
on the surfaces he has exposed – flesh rusting –
and imagines these pieces as they would be

if he left them sitting on this plate
for a day, a week, a month, a year;
how nothing in nature is ugly or wrong.

He cuts the unbitten half in half again
and puts his knife down on the plate,
there, beside his glass of wine-dark wine.

Melbourne Heatwave

Looking straight down from that stone and iron bridge
whose foundations are cushioned into the deep mud
by beds of wool bales from the glory days of sheep
the water is slate-coloured, dense but lively
with its light cargo of occasional soft-drink cans,
bright plastic straws, leaves and the neater leaves
of public transport tickets, and its quickly changing
illegible Arabic-shaped script written in sunlight.
Suddenly a coxless four pierces the cut-off line
like an enlarged but nimble water-surface insect,
surging with each perfect pull of the parallel oars
along the centre of the transformed old river.
The shirtless men have skin almost the same colour
as the boat's wood, and all merge into one entity
so you can't tell if they are rowing or being rowed.
Their oars are dipped with dark green at the flared ends.
They shovel humped water, tilting and jiggling light,
each one turning neatly at the end of its cycle
like a stiff-handed signal from a traffic cop.
The sky is tainted pale with the massive smoke
of bushfires out of control an hour north of here
in the Mount Disappointment State Forest and beyond.
It smells of smoke and wood-ash, nothing else,
but I know that there are houses in there too,
dozens of them gone yesterday and last night
along with their dreams of living in the bush.
I try to imagine what the cities of the future
will smell like when they burn: all those gadgets
flaring and melting into the most dreadful fumes.
A gust out of nowhere flings a plastic shopping bag
into a traffic-light post in a hopeless embrace.
The hot wind reminds me of Rome, the sirocco.
Somewhere among the Roman poets I'd been told
that it brings with it the smell of Africa,
of simooms blasting through the ruins of Carthage.

I had even stopped in the crowded Piazza del Popolo
and optimistically sniffed the summer afternoon breeze
as if there might be some truth in what a poet said.
Another time I stood for hours on the bridge
where Christ broke free of the pack of cults.
There was a drought in Italy and the tawny river
was right down and hardly seemed to flow at all.
It stank like the lane at the back of a restaurant.
You wouldn't have guessed that in Horace's *Odes*
this was a vengeful mass flooding the proud capital.
I talked for a while with an old man beside me
and while we stared into the putrid Tiber
he told me how, not far from here, his son-in-law
had saved a drunken woman who'd fallen in
but that (and here the old man crossed himself)
the poor boy swallowed some of that foul muck
and came down with some terrible disease and died.

Kitchen

In the corner slumps
a sack of spuds,
brown as its contents.

Covered in hernias,
it is hunched over
like an old drunk.

Below the window
freckled with flies,
stands an empty bottle

of homemade grappa,
the kind that creeps up
on you like the devil.

At the far end
of the wooden table
there is an open box

of tissues, one of them
partly standing up
partly folded over

white and triangular
like a stilled yacht
on the horizon.

And at this end
lies the finished letter,
its hilarious news

relayed in lines
so wild they could be
graphs of emotion.

In Memoriam

Eye of the Needle
I.M. Philip Hodgins, 1959-1995

1.

In the earth
there are doorways
from this earth
but they are narrow.

2.

The weight of matter
keeps it down to earth,
as if the property called mass
is store-security, a clip-on
tag-alarm that stops us
taking our garment
when we leave the shop.

3.

Thoughts are already things
before they're set to ink.
Their heaviness is hard
to measure, but material,
being stuff in the head.

Weigh the brain before
and after thinking,
the difference is no
laughing matter, too real
to follow us through Exits.

4.

Even light
is far too heavy.
It must be dark
through there.

Peter Goldsworthy

The Invisible
i.m. Philip Hodgins 1959-1995, our Adonais

As the flight's destination was a country town,
the plane was not much bigger than a bus,
and was driven by propellers – looking down
from my window seat I could see one set of blades,
    seeming blunt-edged as garden spades,
fixed to the wing which would carry all of us.

The propellers started turning, accompanied
by a high-pitched whine, and became at first
two polished blurry discs, before they gathered speed
and disappeared, proving that solids need not be
    visible, as now one could see
through the spinning steel as if through glass. The worst

thing to do would have been to mistake transparency
for lack of substance. The plane was moving
out, as slow as a vehicle in a city
traffic jam, taking its place in a shuffling queue
    of aircraft. A perfect view
was before me, of the giant jetliners leaving

the ground. They would come to a corner at the top
of the runway, with the lumbering, awkward
motion of a circus elephant, and would stop
there for a moment, as if each was a pole-
    vaulter gathering strength, then roll
gently past a marker, and at last rush forward

with astounding momentum, to ascend a ramp
which was as invisible to the eye
as the spinning propeller blades. The tarmac was damp
from morning rain, and on it humans put their trust
    in atoms much smaller than dust-
grains which would raise their luggage into the sky

along with their lives. At once there were tilting fields
in the window's circular frame, followed by
a ridge of houses with swimming pools as shields
beside the tiled helmet-like rooftops. Some horses
        and their stables, green golf courses,
shopping malls, factories, hotels and matchbox-high

office towers rolled under us, before dense cloud
erased the scenery. It was for a while
as though a broadcast had broken down into loud
hissing silence. As we rose, next, into sunlight,
        a dream landscape of endless white
began, sheer vacancy except for a defile

on the horizon which seemed as vague in outline
as the rockery in an aquarium.
After a pause of undecided length, a decline
back through the cushion-stuffing surface of that world
        took place, and below there unfurled
flat fields with dams and windbreaks, and an emporium-

sized hangar surrounded by hedges. The landing
was smooth. We disembarked over the tarmac
and entered a hallway where people were standing
near the door in a loose semi-circle – mourners
        at a graveside. In a corner
my colleague was seated, reading a paperback.

The occasion meant that our greetings were muted.
We got the car, and set off in scotch-mist rain
which eased as we went. A town passed, and fluted
cliffs in the side of a hill, orchards, sheep farms,
        some roadworkers with folded arms,
distant mountains and the vision of sunlit plains.

Though we did not talk much, our thoughts were of the man
whose funeral would be held that day, and to which
we were driving. He had been a friend, and, more than
that, the poet of the countryside the highway
    led us through. In the sky's matte grey
surface there were scrapings of blue steel, and rich

streaks of light fell on tableaus wherein cattle
and gumtrees were disposed as they are on the cover
of his second book. His decade-long battle
with the cancer which consumed his bone-marrow
    had not begun when, at a narrow
table amid a rowdy function, he leaned over

to introduce himself to me. He seemed, then, shy
and modest, and taciturn in manner – who could
have guessed at the conversations which would lie
in our future, leaving the telephone earpiece
    warm as recently slept-in sheets
– and his dress and grooming were such as bespeak good

taste. Yet similar young men were not uncommon,
at the time, and in those circles, so our meeting
was close to dissolving from my recollection
when I saw a piece of his in a magazine
    and thought it especially fine.
A resolve to pass a compliment was fleeting,

as these intentions are, but then a phone-call came
from a mutual friend, with the news about
his leukemia. And so nothing was the same.
No longer was there time for the coincidental
    encounters on which natural
friendship thrives. He had three more years. I sought him out.

We met, and, over lunch, found much compatible
ground in our versions of the true. A decade
younger than me, he made it appear possible
that the follies pursued by my own generation
　　　would be no more than a fashion,
bound for obsolescence. A role he never played,

though he fitted it literally, was the doomed
poet of romance, one of the poses favoured
by those elders. His impatience with the assumed
American style of an indulged middle-class
　　　who, in writing, hoped they might pass
for the outcasts and underdogs of the world, savoured

of plain good sense. Death was stalking him, and was not,
to him, romantic; instead, he resisted
with the nerve of a partisan. Indeed, he fought
so well that the day when he was meant to expire
　　　passed without mishap. The most dire
of forecasts, though proven wrong, still persisted

in overshadowing his life through the next ten
years. We sometimes dared to hope he would survive
us all, so full of life could he seem, yet often
a crisis would develop then pass, false alarms
　　　being part of the disease. Calms
ensued in an ever-changing pattern. Alive,

and vigorous, he joined a group of us to stay
over Christmas in the mountains. The cottage
we borrowed was smothered in creepers, and a grey
pall of neglect filled every room; the garden
　　　was overgrown, with a wooden
pergola fragrant with roses, and a wild patch

of vegetables had seeded by the kitchen door.
After a restless night, we set out walking
on a track which led through ferns and forest before
descending into a gully carved out of stone
    by a cool spilling stream. Alone
in that moss-hung, shadowy place, we started talking

of the need for content in art, of the value
inherent in craft, and of how one conveys
emotion. He knew technique, as each review
would note, as did few other writers, in an age
    when that was shunned. Every page
he worked on was polished and refined over days

through which the words resolved into rightness. They came
out with the sound of his laconic farmer's voice,
obedient to metre and to rhyme. When fame,
of a kind, touched his life, that voice remained unchanged
    although his explorations ranged
over much of the world. Climbing, we had a choice

between two pathways, and took the one which skirted
the face of a cliff. With jagged stone towering
on one side, next to a sheer fall, we were rewarded
by a view toward the valley which lies beyond
    the mountains, like a map opened
at our feet. A blue-tongued lizard and flowering

eucalypts passed by, before we made an ascent
of another rock- and moss-strewn gully, leading
back to the plateau we had set out from. Bent
over and short of breath, I envied him the ease
    with which he climbed, while my stiff knees
stumbled around boulders. Yet his life was bleeding

away, while mine was not. More scenery followed,
chasms, outcrops and waterfalls, and breathtaking
drops protected by wire guard-rails, which swallowed
up the very earth. One such descent had yawned
    before a fugitive, who, warned
to halt by last century's police, preferred making

a leap into the void to the fate of capture.
Gum forest, with its shades of lizard-blue, was hitched
to the horizon, and weathering had made sculpture
out of lichen-stained boulders. His talk revealed
    the schooling from which he was expelled
for a deed still unrepented, memories fetched

back for poems he would later compose. Light ebbed,
and we returned to the cottage with its layers
of dust, its broken, boarded windows and cobwebbed
ceilings, and he cooked a meal we ate in the dim
    dingy kitchen. We learned from him
the strength of resignation. 'Weep for Adonais,'

Shelley wrote of Keats, 'for he is dead.' Yet weeping,
we felt at the time, was unsuited to the humour
he used to face his fate. Tears were not in keeping
for one who wrote about urinals and goannas,
    of football supporters' banners,
and of setting brown snakes loose in a furniture

store. The country of culverts and haybales, of logs
with creatures in them amid the geometry
of empty paddocks, and of cruelty to dogs
as casual as kindness, accepted the fact
    of death, like the sexual act,
and took it for granted. Driving through that country,

we felt as if his living presence filled it yet.
The time for the funeral was now approaching,
but we still had to reach the town where it was set.
We had tried a short cut which became a detour
	through a preserved mining town, pure
as a Disney construction. My friend, reproaching

himself for the delay, had worked up a fever
of misdirected guilt and near-rage. A railway
bridge at the outskirts ended his fears, whatever
they were, and we arrived in time for the cortege
	to be arranged. Beyond the edge
of town there were old mine-workings, in fields as grey

as the craters on an asteroid, and the cars
processed through this landscape in a slow-moving file
like the aircraft lining up on a runway. Scars
of the gold-rush era were punctuated by fields
	where cattle grazed the barren yields,
while suburban-seeming houses appeared each mile.

Then the procession turned through a nondescript
gate, and a few scattered headstones could be seen
on the slope of a low hill, among the leaf-stripped
trunks of tall trees which resembled telegraph posts
	in their rigid uprightness, most
of their height beneath a cluster of olive-green

leafage being bare enough for light to flood
the ground. A crowd of people stood among those trees,
in a half-circle facing a hole dug through mud
and strata of clay and stone. Many had faces
	I had known from other places.
They stayed silent, though a cockatoo broke the peace

with its harsh call. Then the hearse – a humble station-
wagon – appeared, and four men hoisted a varnished
pine coffin onto their shoulders. Concentration
focussed on them until the silence broke again
    with the sound of a woman's pain:
it was his widow sobbing, a pure, ungarnished,

heartfelt cry which made us envision our friend, laid
out as though asleep, within that brass-handled box;
her tears brought to mind his sardonic, well-made
face, his eyes and voice and limbs, which to her had meant
    more than to any of us, spent
and vacant now, descending past layers of rocks

without return. Something invisible had fled
from him, and now a mechanical hoist lowered
what was left from view. *Weep for Adonais, he is dead.*
Meanwhile, his children played among gravestones as though
    at a picnic, oblivious, so
it would seem, to their mother's grief. Motor-powered,

the slow descent came to an end, accompanied
by a rending groan which could have been the lid
prised open from within. But there was no need
for thoughts of resurrection. Instead of a priest,
    poets began what was his last
reading: *That is no country for old men.* He did

not want consolation for his friends, and neither
did he expect a soothing ceremony
to attend his burial. There is no life other
than that of words on paper, he believed, to look
    forward to. A loud chicken's squawk
from a farmyard nearby upset the dignity

of the occasion, but only for an instant,
reminding us all of life's continuation
in rose-bordered bungalows where a shrub's pleasant
scent overwhelms the fragrance from the poultry shed.
        Everything one could have said
was finished. We returned, as to the reception

after a wedding, to a room with sausages
impaled on toothpicks, asparagus rolls, warm pies,
and cakes and cups of tea, while light-filled passages
with polished hardwood floors reverberated
        to the kind of talk he hated
to miss. At length my colleague said his goodbyes

on both of our behalf. Even though the afternoon
was close to passing, he intended to drive home.
We retraced our journey in waning light, which soon
became pitch darkness, and swept through swamps we
                could smell
        without seeing, towns with one hotel
and a single street-lamp, and ghost-gums white as foam

were caught in the headlights. By dinner we had reached
a country town which resembled an outer
suburb transplanted into a vast plain of bleached
pastureland: its flag-bedecked car-dealers' yards,
        supermarkets with discount cards,
floodlit takeaways, video stores, and utter

blankness of character, was less than inviting.
Fuelled by coffee, we continued to drive.
Time was passing, and already we were fighting
sleep, on the featureless road which unreeled toward
        the river flats at the border.
There were no other cars. The only ones alive,

that night, were hidden away, behind the porch lights
glowing out of farms which were lost among clumps of trees
the moonless sky revealed in silhouette. Such nights
of ceaseless driving are blurred in recollection
    and half-real, for each impression
is succeeded by an unrelated scene. Skies

smudged with cloud parted on a star-cluttered dome,
like a conjuror's glitter costume, while we wound
among the elephant-like trunks of river red-gum
forest and the clay banks of silent waterways.
    At midnight, we crossed a black space
in the ground, which was the river's channel, and turned

along a gravel-edged cutting through the folded hills
away from the main road. Another short-cut. Bowl-
shaped valleys, each one brimming with mist, as one fills
a pet's dish with milk. At first the pale liquid cleared
    with the next rise, but more appeared
in every crease of the land. A creekbed's whole

length would be trimmed with cloud. It was, soon, no
            mere mist
which covered all of the hollows like a blanket;
it was a fog as thick as the smoke-skeins which twist
from the chimneys of kilns. The road vanished from view
    before our eyes; we drove on through
a shroud, transformed by an artist's monotone palette.

It was like being in the plane as it pushed through
the cloud-ceiling, earlier that day; an ideal
landscape, upholstered in white, appeared when we flew
over hill-crests, but then we would dive again, and crawl
    blindly through fog which was for all
the world like encroaching cataracts. We would feel,

through those long moments, as one does in a nightmare
of helplessness, and each new wave breaking over
us was like the sleep which was threatening to tear
down our wakefulness. The scale of time seemed altered
     as it is in flight; and we faltered,
groping, as the wheels churned up gravel and clover

from the verge before righting themselves. The stars
above us excepted, there were no lights, no farms
or railway sidings, and nor were there passing cars,
so a town came as a surprise, out of the mist.
     A few dark houses, a signpost,
and we came upon a main street with all the charms

of a former time's architecture: verandahs
over paved sidewalks, closed wooden shutters, and rails
for horses – empty as expected in the hour
after midnight. The fog swirled over a street-lamp
     like ectoplasm. An air of damp
unreality, as though upon the stage. Veils

of mist hiding the side-streets; a drinking-trough;
shopfronts with simple lettering – BUTCHER, GROCER,
and GENERAL STORE; a feeble light winking off
behind a curtained window; no petrol station,
     no sign of modernisation,
though all of the town seemed newly made; buildings closer

together than in the outspread suburbs of our
age. In a film, or in someone's novel, a trap-
door would have opened next, on a strange adventure
through unknown dimensions; instead, nothing happened,
     and we went on by the flattened
metal ruins in a car-wrecker's yard, a flap

of canvas pulled over old motor parts, and past
the town's last cottages and sheds. The dark country
resumed, and still each declivity breathed out mist:
at one point it was shoulder-deep, so that our heads
    skimmed over whiteness like a bed's,
in air clear as springwater, under symmetry

of stars. The ground started rising, at length, and less
cloud covered the road, which grew wider and more smooth.
Gateposts and other traces of populousness,
such as road-signs and letter-boxes, could be seen
    in the headlights' duplicate beam.
A radio transmission tower, a sharp tooth

outlined against the stars, and plantations of pines
and poplars – and then a reflective green placard
announced the main highway. Suddenly there were lines
of traffic, even though we were in the middle
    hours of night, so for a little
while we had to pause at the junction to let hard-

driven transport-convoys sweep up the hill, with lights
strung like yuletide decorations on each trailer;
after hours of darkness, the effect of this sight
was as of coming to a shining and noble
    city amid the wild – mobile,
luminous, roaring; or of landfall for a sailor

approaching Byzantium. It was the city
of the future, it almost seemed, where emotion
will be replaced by machines, and technology
on wheels rule all our desires. We had left the past
    behind, in the mist, moving fast,
and police cars prowled like sharks beneath the ocean.

Jamie Grant

Philip Hodgins (1959–1995)

Your funeral recalled for me your poems;
I seemed to feel your touch about it all –
sparse trees nearby, sinuous, stringy gums,
their leaves, rags on barbed wire; the lustrous call
of furious magpies; clay instead of tombs;
and low weather, with dry weeds and thistle
that we came wandering over, scatteredly,
to the coffin, strung above its cavity.

The empty place the world is hung upon.
'No speeches, only verse,' in your dicta.
I read one of those pieces you had chosen,
'Sailing To Byzantium'. How bitter
the humour, the irony, you'd added. Then,
because there'd dried up here part of the delta
of the Murray, it seemed right that Les spoke –
spontaneously brilliant, a common bloke.

Hartley and Paul read briefly. That was all.
Backyards of wooden houses, fairly near.
Each of us threw into the eight-foot hole
a flower. But first, had to stand and hear
ropes slowly creak, unwound from a steel rail –
a labour to breathe, stopping; heads bowed there.
At a mullock heap, along that gravel track,
out in Victoria, something gold put back

Just nights before your twelve-year fight was up
you rang. 'Tell them I was a great hater,'
you said. The Literature Board's lucky-dip,
demoralising to a true writer;
feminists' self-pitying career; French slop,
that only 'signs' exist (hearts of water);
treasonous clerks in the university …
condemning these you'd call your best elegy.

You were as loyal as a classic Roman;
vehement and pure; a believer in style;
stoic, yet glamorous like Wilfred Owen;
the exemplar of an Australian school –
going straight for the pay-dirt of emotion,
laconic, pragmatic and sceptical.
'Live another thirty years!' If I do,
it'll seem a moment, then. I'll think of you.

Robert Gray

Blue Roan
For Philip Hodgins

As usual up the Giro mountain
dozers were shifting the road about
but the big blue ranges looked permanent
and the stinging-trees held no hint of drought.

All the high drill and blanket ridges
were dusty for want of winter rains
but down in the creases of picnic oak
brown water moved like handled chains.

Steak-red Herefords, edged like steaks
with that creamy fat the health trade bars
nudged, feeding, settling who'd get horned
and who'd horn, in the Wingham abattoirs

and men who remembered droughttime grass
like three days' growth on a stark red face
described farms on the creeks, fruit trees and fun
and how they bought out each little place.

Where farm families once would come just to watch
men knock off work, on the Bulliac line,
the fear of helplessness still burned live brush.
Dirty white smoke sent up its scattered sign

and in at the races and out at home
the pump of morale was primed and bled:
'Poor Harry in the street, beer running out his eyes,'
as the cousin who married the baker said.

Les Murray

Index of Titles